30
Essential
Lessons
from
Proverbs

Freeman-Smith, a division of Worthy Media, Inc.
134 Franklin Road, Suite 200, Brentwood, Tennessee 37027

The quoted ideas expressed in this book (but not Scripture verses) are not, in all cases, exact quotations, as some have been edited for clarity and brevity. In all cases, the author has attempted to maintain the speaker's original intent. In some cases, quoted material for this book was obtained from secondary sources, primarily print media. While every effort was made to ensure the accuracy of these sources, the accuracy cannot be guaranteed. For additions, deletions, corrections, or clarifications in future editions of this text, please write Freeman-Smith.

Scripture quotations are taken from:

The Holy Bible, King James Version

The Holy Bible, New International Version (NIV) Copyright © 1973, 1978, 1984, by International Bible Society. Used by permission of Zondervan Publishing House. All rights reserved.

The Holy Bible, New King James Version (NKJV) Copyright © 1982 by Thomas Nelson, Inc. Used by permission.

The Holy Bible, New Living Translation, (NLT) Copyright © 1996. Used by permission of Tyndale House Publishers, Inc., Wheaton, Illinois 60189. All rights reserved.

The New American Standard Bible®, (NASB) Copyright © 1960, 1962, 1963, 1968, 1971, 1972, 1973, 1975, 1977, 1995 by The Lockman Foundation. Used by permission.

The Message (MSG)- This edition issued by contractual arrangement with NavPress, a division of The Navigators, U.S.A. Originally published by NavPress in English as THE MESSAGE: The Bible in Contemporary Language copyright 2002-2003 by Eugene Peterson. All rights reserved.

The Holman Christian Standard Bible™ (HCSB) Copyright © 1999, 2000, 2001 by Holman Bible Publishers. Used by permission.

Cover Design by Kim Russell / Wahoo Designs
Page Layout by Bart Dawson

ISBN 978-1-60587-342-8

Printed in the United States of America

30
Essential
Lessons
from
Proverbs

Table of Contents

Introduction

How desperately our world needs wise Christians who are willing to honor God with their prayers and their service. This generation faces problems that defy easy solutions, yet face them we must. We need leaders whose vision is clear and whose intentions are pure. Hopefully, you are determined to become such a person—a faithful servant who walks in wisdom as he offers counsel and direction to family, to friends, and to coworkers.

The fabric of daily life is woven together with the threads of habit, and no habit is more important than that of consistent prayer and daily devotion to the Creator. And this book is intended to help. This text contains 30 chapters, each of which contains an essential lesson from the Book of Proverbs. During the next 30 days, please try this experiment: read a chapter from this book each day. If you're already committed to a daily time of worship, this book will enrich that experience. If you are not, the simple act of giving God a few minutes each morning will change the direction of your day and the quality of your life.

About the Book of Proverbs and You

The Book of Proverbs, which was authored hundreds of years before the birth of Christ, is as relevant today as it was on the day it was written. In fact, Proverbs contains indispensable advice that you, as Christian men and women living in the 21st century, should apply to the everyday realities of your life. Proverbs teaches you where to find wisdom, how to use it, and how to share it.

As you consider the wisdom of King Solomon, the primary author of the text, as well as the contributions of Agur and Lemuel, men who supplied later additions, please remember that God's wisdom never grows old.

Do you place a high value on the acquisition of wisdom? If so, you are not alone; most men and women would like to be wise, but not all are willing to do the work that is required to become wise. Wisdom is not like a mushroom; it does not spring up overnight. It is, instead, like an oak tree that starts as a tiny acorn, grows into a sapling, and eventually reaches up to the sky, tall and strong.

To become wise, you must seek God's guidance with consistency and purpose. And a wonderful way to discern His guidance is by beginning a lifelong study of the eternal truths found in Proverbs.

Lesson 1

Mountain-Moving Faith

Trust in the LORD with all thine heart;
and lean not unto thine own understanding.

Proverbs 3:5 KJV

THE LESSON

Always trust God. When you have faith in Him—and when you act accordingly—you can move mountains.

Because we live in a demanding world, all of us have mountains to climb and mountains to move. Moving those mountains requires faith. And the experience of trying, with God's help, to move mountains builds character.

Faith, like a tender seedling, can be nurtured or neglected. When we nurture our faith through prayer, meditation, and worship, God blesses our lives and lifts our spirits. But when we neglect to commune with the Father, we do ourselves and our loved ones a profound disservice.

Are you a mountain-mover whose faith is evident for all to see? Or, are you a spiritual underachiever? As you think about the answer to that question, consider this: God needs more people who are willing to move mountains for His glory and for His kingdom.

> Only God can move mountains, but faith and prayer can move God.
>
> —
>
> *E. M. Bounds*

Every life—including yours— is a series of wins and losses. Every step of the way, through every triumph and tragedy, God walks with you, ready and willing to strengthen you. So the next time you find your character being tested, remember to take your fears to God. If you call upon Him, you will be comforted. Whatever your challenge, whatever your trouble, God can handle it.

When you place your faith, your trust, and your life in the hands of your Heavenly Father, you'll receive a lesson in character-building from the ultimate Teacher. So strengthen your faith through praise, through worship, through Bible study, and through prayer. And trust God's plans. With Him, all things are possible, and He stands ready to open a world of possibilities to you . . . if you have faith.

SOMETHING TO THINK ABOUT

Today, think about the times you've been hesitant to share your faith. And as you contemplate the day ahead, think about three specific ways that you can vocalize your faith to family and friends.

Faith is confidence in the promises of God or confidence that God will do what He has promised.

Charles Stanley

As we seek to become disciples of Jesus Christ, we should never forget that the word disciple is directly related to the word discipline. To be a disciple of the Lord Jesus Christ is to know his discipline.

Dennis Swanberg

There is not Christianity without a cross, for you cannot be a disciple of Jesus without taking up your cross.

Henry Blackaby

I do not want merely to possess a faith; I want a faith that possesses me.

Charles Kingsley

How do you walk in faith? By claiming the promises of God and obeying the Word of God, in spite of what you see, how you feel, or what may happen.

Warren Wiersbe

MORE FROM GOD'S WORD

I assure you: If anyone says to this mountain, "Be lifted up and thrown into the sea," and does not doubt in his heart, but believes that what he says will happen, it will be done for him.

Mark 11:23 HCSB

For whatever is born of God overcomes the world. And this is the victory that has overcome the world—our faith.

1 John 5:4 NKJV

Now without faith it is impossible to please God, for the one who draws near to Him must believe that He exists and rewards those who seek Him.

Hebrews 11:6 HCSB

Everything is possible to the one who believes.

Mark 9:23 HCSB

Pursue righteousness, godliness, faith, love, endurance, and gentleness. Fight the good fight for the faith; take hold of eternal life, to which you were called and have made a good confession before many witnesses.

1 Timothy 6:11-12 HCSB

MY THOUGHTS ON THIS LESSON

_____

_____

_____

_____

_____

_____

_____

_____

_____

A PRAYER

Dear Lord, I want faith that moves mountains. You have big plans
for this world and big plans for me. Help me fulfill those plans,
Father, as I follow in the footsteps of Your Son. Amen

Lesson 2

He Wants
to Guide You

In all your ways acknowledge Him,
and He shall direct your paths.

Proverbs 3:6 NKJV

THE LESSON

God will guide you if you let Him. You job is to acknowledge
Him and to follow closely in the footsteps of His Son.

The Bible promises that God will guide you if you let Him. Your job, of course, is to let Him. But sometimes, you will be tempted to do otherwise. Sometimes, you'll be tempted to go along with the crowd; other times, you'll be tempted to do things your way, not God's way. When you feel those temptations, you must resist them, or else.

What will you allow to guide you through the coming day: your own desires (or, for that matter, the desires of your peers)? Or will you allow God to lead the way? The answer should be obvious. You should let God be your guide. When you entrust your life to Him completely and without reservation, God will give you the strength to meet any challenge, the courage to face any trial, and the wisdom to live in His righteousness. So trust Him today and seek His guidance. When you do, your character will most certainly take care of itself, and your next step will most assuredly be the right one.

SOMETHING TO THINK ABOUT

Would you like God's guidance? Then ask Him for it. When you pray for guidance, God will give it. So ask.

Fix your eyes upon the Lord! Do it once. Do it daily. Do it constantly. Look at the Lord and keep looking at Him.

Charles Swindoll

We are either the masters or the victims of our attitudes. It is a matter of personal choice. Who we are today is the result of choices we made yesterday. Tomorrow, we will become what we choose today. To change means to choose to change.

John Maxwell

God's plan for our guidance is for us to grow gradually in wisdom before we get to the crossroads.

Bill Hybels

Are you serious about wanting God's guidance to become a personal reality in your life? The first step is to tell God that you know you can't manage your own life; that you need his help.

Catherine Marshall

Only He can guide you to invest your life in worthwhile ways. This guidance will come as you "walk" with Him and listen to Him.

Henry Blackaby and Claude King

We must always invite Jesus to be the navigator of our plans, desires, wills, and emotions, for He is the way, the truth, and the life.

Bill Bright

Life is a series of choices between the bad, the good, and the best. Everything depends on how we choose.

Vance Havner

Good and evil both increase at compound interest. That is why the little decisions you and I make every day are of such infinite importance.

C. S. Lewis

Every day, I find countless opportunities to decide whether I will obey God and demonstrate my love for Him or try to please myself or the world system. God is waiting for my choices.

Bill Bright

Life is pretty much like a cafeteria line—it offers us many choices, both good and bad. The Christian must have a spiritual radar that detects the difference not only between bad and good but also among good, better, and best.

Dennis Swanberg

MORE FROM GOD'S WORD

He awakens [Me] each morning; He awakens My ear to listen like those being instructed. The Lord God has opened My ear, and I was not rebellious; I did not turn back.

Isaiah 50:4-5 HCSB

The thing you should want most is God's kingdom and doing what God wants. Then all these other things you need will be given to you.

Matthew 6:33 NCV

Yet Lord, You are our Father; we are the clay, and You are our potter; we all are the work of Your hands.

Isaiah 64:8 HCSB

When people do not accept divine guidance, they run wild. But whoever obeys the law is happy.

Proverbs 29:18 NLT

Lord, You light my lamp; my God illuminates my darkness.

Psalm 18:28 HCSB

MY THOUGHTS ON THIS LESSON

_____

_____

_____

_____

_____

_____

_____

_____

_____

A PRAYER

Dear Lord, thank You for Your constant presence and
Your constant love. I draw near to You this day with the
confidence that You are ready to guide me. Help me walk closely
with You, Father, and help me share Your Good News
with all who cross my path. Amen

Lesson 3

Studying His Word

*Every word of God is pure: he is a shield
unto them that put their trust in him.*

Proverbs 30:5 KJV

THE LESSON

God's Word is a shield to those who trust it, study it, and
obey it.

I s Bible study a high priority for you? The answer to this simple question will determine, to a surprising extent, the quality of your life and the direction of your faith.

As you establish priorities for life, you must decide whether God's Word will be a bright spotlight that guides your path every day or a tiny nightlight that occasionally flickers in the dark. The decision to study the Bible—or not—is yours and yours alone. But make no mistake: how you choose to use your Bible will have a profound impact on you and your loved ones.

George Mueller observed, "The vigor of our spiritual lives will be in exact proportion to the place held by the Bible in our lives and in our thoughts." Think of it like this: the more you use your Bible, the more God will use you.

Perhaps you're one of those Christians who owns a bookshelf full of unread Bibles. If so, remember the old saying, "A Bible in the hand is worth two in the bookcase." Or perhaps you're one of those folks who is simply "too busy" to find time for a daily dose of prayer and Bible study. If so, remember the old adage, "It's hard to stumble when you're on your knees."

God's Word can be a roadmap to a place of righteousness and abundance. Make it your roadmap. God's wisdom can be a light to guide your steps. Claim it as your light today, tomorrow, and every day of your life—and then walk confidently in the footsteps of God's only begotten Son.

SOMETHING TO THINK ABOUT

The Bible is God's roadmap for life here on earth and for life eternal. How you choose to use your Bible is, of course, up to you . . . and so are the consequences. So today, challenge your faith by making sure that you're spending quality time each day studying God's Word.

Nobody ever outgrows Scripture; the book widens and deepens with our years.

C. H. Spurgeon

There is a glorified Man on the right hand of the Majesty in heaven faithfully representing us there. We are left for a season among men; let us faithfully represent Him here.

A. W. Tozer

I study the Bible as I gather apples. First, I shake the whole tree that the ripest might fall. Then I shake each limb; I shake each branch and every twig. Then, I look under every leaf.

Martin Luther

Study the Bible and observe how the persons behaved and how God dealt with them. There is explicit teaching on every condition of life.

Corrie ten Boom

Only through routine, regular exposure to God's Word can you and I draw out the nutrition needed to grow a heart of faith.

Elizabeth George

If you want to know God as he speaks to you through the Bible, you should study the Bible daily, systematically, comprehensively, devotionally, and prayerfully.

James Montgomery Boice

The vigor of our spiritual lives will be in exact proportion to the place held by the Bible in our lives and in our thoughts.

George Mueller

Although our actions have nothing to do with gaining our own salvation, they might be used by God to save somebody else! What we do really matters, and it can affect the eternities of people we care about.

Bill Hybels

MORE FROM GOD'S WORD

Man shall not live by bread alone, but by every word that proceeds from the mouth of God.

Matthew 4:4 NKJV

You will be a good servant of Christ Jesus, constantly nourished on the words of the faith and of the sound doctrine which you have been following.

1 Timothy 4:6 NASB

But grow in the grace and knowledge of our Lord and Savior Jesus Christ. To Him be the glory both now and forever. Amen.

2 Peter 3:18 NKJV

There's nothing like the written Word of God for showing you the way to salvation through faith in Christ Jesus. Every part of Scripture is God-breathed and useful one way or another, showing us truth, exposing our rebellion, correcting our mistakes, training us to live God's way. Through the Word we are put together and shaped up for the tasks God has for us.

2 Timothy 3:15-17 MSG

For I am not ashamed of the gospel of Christ, for it is the power of God to salvation for everyone who believes.

Romans 1:16 NKJV

My Thoughts on This Lesson

_____

_____

_____

_____

_____

_____

_____

_____

_____

_____

A Prayer

Heavenly Father, You have given me the gift of Your Holy Word.
Let me study it, and let me live according to its principles.
Let me read Your Word, meditate upon it, and share its joyous
message with the world, today and every day. Amen

Lesson 4

Share Your Enthusiasm

A joyful heart is good medicine,
but a broken spirit dries up the bones.
Proverbs 17:22 NASB

THE LESSON

A joyful, enthusiastic heart is a blessing from the Creator.

Are you passionate about your faith, your life, your family, and your future? Hopefully so. But if your zest for life has waned, it is now time to redirect your efforts and recharge your spiritual batteries. And that means refocusing your priorities by putting God first.

Each day is a glorious opportunity to serve God and to do His will. Are you enthused about life, or do you struggle through each day giving scarcely a thought to God's blessings? Are you constantly praising God for His gifts, and are you sharing His Good News with the world? And are you excited about the possibilities for service that God has placed before you, whether at home, at work, or at church? You should be.

Nothing is more important than your wholehearted commitment to your Creator and to His only begotten Son. Your faith must never be an afterthought; it must be your ultimate priority, your ultimate possession, and your ultimate passion. When you become passionate about your faith, you'll become passionate about your life, too.

Norman Vincent Peale advised, "Get absolutely enthralled with something. Throw yourself into it with abandon. Get out of yourself. Be somebody. Do something." His words apply to you. So don't settle for a lukewarm existence. Instead, make the choice to become genuinely involved in life. The world needs your enthusiasm . . . and so do you.

SOMETHING TO THINK ABOUT

Don't wait for enthusiasm to find you . . . go looking for it. Look at your life and your relationships as exciting adventures. Don't wait for life to spice itself up; spice things up yourself.

When we wholeheartedly commit ourselves to God, there is nothing mediocre or run-of-the-mill about us. To live for Christ is to be passionate about our Lord and about our lives.

Jim Gallery

Success or failure can be pretty well predicted by the degree to which the heart is fully in it.

John Eldredge

We honor God by asking for great things when they are part of His promise. We dishonor Him and cheat ourselves when we ask for molehills where He has offered mountains.

Vance Havner

Wherever you are, be all there. Live to the hilt every situation you believe to be the will of God.

Jim Elliot

Catch on fire with enthusiasm and people will come for miles to watch you burn.

John Wesley

One of the great needs in the church today is for every Christian to become enthusiastic about his faith in Jesus Christ.

Billy Graham

It is a remarkable thing that some of the most optimistic and enthusiastic people you will meet are those who have been through intense suffering.

Warren Wiersbe

Enthusiasm, like the flu, is contagious—we get it from one another.

Barbara Johnson

Don't take hold of a thing unless you want that thing to take hold of you.

E. Stanley Jones

MORE FROM GOD'S WORD

Whatever you do, do it enthusiastically, as something done for the Lord and not for men.

Colossians 3:23 HCSB

Do not lack diligence; be fervent in spirit; serve the Lord.

Romans 12:11 HCSB

Whatever your hands find to do, do with [all] your strength.

Ecclesiastes 9:10 HCSB

I have seen that there is nothing better than for a person to enjoy his activities, because that is his reward. For who can enable him to see what will happen after he dies?

Ecclesiastes 3:22 HCSB

Don't work only while being watched, in order to please men, but as slaves of Christ, do God's will from your heart. Render service with a good attitude, as to the Lord and not to men.

Ephesians 6:6-7 HCSB

MY THOUGHTS ON THIS LESSON

A PRAYER

Dear Lord, You have called me not to a life of mediocrity,
but to a life of passion. Today, I will be an enthusiastic follower
of Your Son, and I will share His Good News—and His love—
with all who cross my path. Amen

Lesson 5

The Importance of Integrity

The one who lives with integrity lives securely,
but whoever perverts his ways will be found out.

Proverbs 10:9 HCSB

THE LESSON

God's Word promises that honesty will be rewarded and dishonesty will be punished.

Billy Graham correctly observed, "Integrity is the glue that holds our way of life together. We must constantly strive to keep our integrity intact. When wealth is lost, nothing is lost; when health is lost, something is lost; when character is lost, all is lost." Yet all too often, we find it far more convenient to be dishonest with ourselves, with our loved ones, and with our Father in heaven. And the results can be heartbreaking.

As Christians we are called to walk with God and to obey His commandments. But, we live in a world that presents us with countless temptations to wander far from God's path. These temptations have the potential to destroy us, in part, because they cause us to be dishonest with ourselves and with others.

> Character is what you are in the dark.
>
> —
>
> *D. L. Moody*

Dishonesty is a habit. Once we start bending the truth, we're likely to keep bending it. A far better strategy, of course, is to acquire the habit of being completely forthright with God, with other people, and with ourselves.

Honesty, like its counterpart, is also a habit, a habit that pays powerful dividends for those who place character above convenience. So, make this simple promise to yourself and keep it: when you're tempted to bend the truth, even slightly—or to break it— ask yourself this question: "What does God want me to do?" Then listen carefully to your conscience. When you do, your actions will be honorable, and your character will take care of itself.

> ## SOMETHING TO THINK ABOUT
>
> Take time to think about your own character, both your strong points and your weaknesses. Then list three aspects of your character—longstanding habits or troublesome behaviors—that you would like to modify. Finally, ask God to be your partner as you take steps to improve yourself and your life.

Before God changes our circumstances, He wants to change our hearts.

Warren Wiersbe

There's nothing like the power of integrity. It is a characteristic so radiant, so steady, so consistent, so beautiful, that it makes a permanent picture in our minds.

Franklin Graham

Maintaining your integrity in a world of sham is no small accomplishment.

Wayne Oates

Every time you refuse to face up to life and its problems, you weaken your character.

E. Stanley Jones

No man can use his Bible with power unless he has the character of Jesus in his heart.

Alan Redpath

Right actions done for the wrong reason do not help to build the internal quality of character called a "virtue," and it is this quality or character that really matters.

C. S. Lewis

A little lie is like a little pregnancy. It doesn't take long before everyone knows.

C. S. Lewis

God loves you, and He yearns for you to turn away from the path of evil. You need His forgiveness, and you need Him to come into your life and remake you from within.

Billy Graham

MORE FROM GOD'S WORD

Blessed is the man who walks not in the counsel of the ungodly, nor stands in the path of sinners, nor sits in the seat of the scornful; but his delight is in the law of the Lord, and in His law he meditates day and night. He shall be like a tree planted by the rivers of water, that brings forth its fruit in its season, whose leaf also shall not wither; and whatever he does shall prosper.

Psalm 1:1-3 NKJV

Don't ever forget kindness and truth. Wear them like a necklace. Write them on your heart as if on a tablet.

Proverbs 3:3 NCV

In all things showing yourself to be a pattern of good works; in doctrine showing integrity, reverence, incorruptibility . . . .

Titus 2:7 NKJV

Lead a quiet and peaceable life in all godliness and honesty.

1 Timothy 2:2 KJV

We also rejoice in our afflictions, because we know that affliction produces endurance, endurance produces proven character, and proven character produces hope.

Romans 5:3-4 HCSB

MY THOUGHTS ON THIS LESSON

_____

_____

_____

_____

_____

_____

_____

_____

_____

_____

_____

A PRAYER

Dear Lord, every day can be an exercise in character-building, and that's what I intend to make this day. I will be mindful that my thoughts and actions have great consequences, consequences in my own life and in the lives of my loved ones. I will strive to make my thoughts and actions pleasing to You, so that I may be an instrument of Your peace, today and every day. Amen

Lesson 6

He Has a Plan for You

Commit your activities to the Lord
and your plans will be achieved.
Proverbs 16:3 HCSB

THE LESSON

When you commit your plans to God—and when you follow
through on those plans with determination and obedience—
you will be blessed.

"What did God put me here to do?" If you're like most people, you've asked yourself that question on many occasions. Perhaps you have pondered your future, uncertain of your plans, unsure of your next step. But even if you don't have a clear plan for the next step of your life's journey, you may rest assured that God does.

God has a plan for the universe, and He has a plan for you. He understands that plan as thoroughly and completely as He knows you. If you seek God's will earnestly and prayerfully, He will make His plans known to you in His own time and in His own way.

Do you sincerely seek to discover God's purpose for your life? If so, you must first be willing to live in accordance with His commandments. You must also study God's Word and be watchful for His signs. Finally, you should open yourself up to the Creator every day—beginning with this one—and you must have faith that He will soon reveal His plans to you.

> You cannot out-dream God.
>
> —
>
> *John Eldredge*

Perhaps your vision of God's purpose for your life has been clouded by a wish list that you have expected God to dutifully fulfill. Perhaps, you have fervently hoped that God would create a world that unfolds according to your wishes, not His. If so, you have experienced more disappointment than satisfaction and more frustration than peace. A better strategy is to conform your will to God's (and not to struggle vainly in an attempt to conform His will to yours).

Sometimes, God's plans and purposes may seem unmistakably clear to you. If so, push ahead. But other times, He may lead you through the wilderness before He directs you to the Promised Land. So be patient and keep seeking His will for your life. When you do, you'll be amazed at the marvelous things that an all-powerful, all-knowing God can do.

SOMETHING TO THINK ABOUT

Perhaps you're in a hurry to understand God's unfolding plan for your life. If so, remember that God operates according to a perfect timetable. That timetable is His, not yours. So be patient. God has big things in store for you, but He may have quite a few lessons to teach you before you are fully prepared to do His will and fulfill His purpose.

We must focus on prayer as the main thrust to accomplish God's will and purpose on earth. The forces against us have never been greater, and this is the only way we can release God's power to become victorious.

John Maxwell

You were born with tremendous potential. When you were born again through faith in Jesus Christ, God added spiritual gifts to your natural talents.

Warren Wiersbe

When God speaks to you through the Bible, prayer, circumstances, the church, or in some other way, he has a purpose in mind for your life.

Henry Blackaby and Claude King

The greatest tragedy is not death, but life without purpose.

Rick Warren

Let us live with urgency. Let us exploit the opportunity of life. Let us not drift. Let us live intentionally. We must not trifle our lives away.

Raymond Ortlund

MORE FROM GOD'S WORD

He is the image of the invisible God, the firstborn over all creation; because by Him everything was created, in heaven and on earth, the visible and the invisible, whether thrones or dominions or rulers or authorities—all things have been created through Him and for Him.

Colossians 1:15-16 HCSB

For it is God who is working among you both the willing and the working for His good purpose.

Philippians 2:13 HCSB

We know that all things work together for the good of those who love God: those who are called according to His purpose.

Romans 8:28 HCSB

I will instruct you and show you the way to go; with My eye on you, I will give counsel.

Psalm 32:8 HCSB

You reveal the path of life to me; in Your presence is abundant joy; in Your right hand are eternal pleasures.

Psalm 16:11 HCSB

My Thoughts on This Lesson

_____

_____

_____

_____

_____

_____

_____

_____

_____

_____

A Prayer

Dear Lord, let Your purposes be my purposes.
Let Your priorities be my priorities. Let Your will be my will.
Let Your Word be my guide. And, let me grow in faith and in
wisdom today and every day. Amen

Lesson 7

A Willingness to Serve

The one who blesses others is abundantly blessed;
those who help others are helped.

Proverbs 11:25 MSG

THE LESSON

God calls you to a life of service. When you serve Him with
gladness, you will be blessed.

We live in a world that glorifies power, prestige, fame, and money. But the words of Jesus teach us that the most esteemed men and women are not the widely acclaimed leaders of society; the most esteemed among us are the humble servants of society.

Dietrich Bonhoeffer was correct when he observed, "It is very easy to overestimate the importance of our own achievements in comparison with what we owe others." In other words, reality breeds humility . . . and humility should breed service.

Every single day of your life, including this one, God will give you opportunities to serve Him by serving other people. Welcome those opportunities with open arms. Always be willing to pitch in and make the world a better place, and forego the temptation to keep all your blessings to yourself. When you do, you'll earn rewards that are simply unavailable to folks who stubbornly refuse to serve.

> We are never more like God than when we give.
>
> —
>
> *Charles Swindoll*

Service is a character-building experience: the more you serve, the more you grow. So, as you go about your daily activities, remember this: the Savior of all humanity made Himself a servant . . . and if you want to really know Him better, you must do the same.

SOMETHING TO THINK ABOUT

Whatever your age, whatever your circumstances, you can serve: Each stage of life's journey is a glorious opportunity to place yourself in the service of the One who is the Giver of all blessings. As long as you live, you should honor God with your service to others.

In Jesus, the service of God and the service of the least of the brethren were one.

Dietrich Bonhoeffer

Nothing is really ours until we share it.

C. S. Lewis

If you want to be truly happy, you won't find it on an endless quest for more stuff. You'll find it in receiving God's generosity and in passing that generosity along.

Bill Hybels

If you aren't serving, you're just existing, because life is meant for ministry.

Rick Warren

If doing a good act in public will excite others to do more good, then "Let your Light shine to all." Miss no opportunity to do good.

John Wesley

God does not do anything with us, only through us.

Oswald Chambers

In the very place where God has put us, whatever its limitations, whatever kind of work it may be, we may indeed serve the Lord Christ.

Elisabeth Elliot

Doing something positive toward another person is a practical approach to feeling good about yourself.

Barbara Johnson

Through our service to others, God wants to influence our world for Him.

Vonette Bright

MORE FROM GOD'S WORD

For I have given you an example that you also should do just as I have done for you.

John 13:15 HCSB

Therefore, get your minds ready for action, being self-disciplined, and set your hope completely on the grace to be brought to you at the revelation of Jesus Christ.

1 Peter 1:13 HCSB

Now there are different gifts, but the same Spirit. There are different ministries, but the same Lord.

1 Corinthians 12:4-5 HCSB

Therefore, since we are receiving a kingdom that cannot be shaken, let us hold on to grace. By it, we may serve God acceptably, with reverence and awe.

Hebrews 12:28 HCSB

If they serve Him obediently, they will end their days in prosperity and their years in happiness.

Job 36:11 HCSB

My Thoughts on This Lesson

_____

_____

_____

_____

_____

_____

_____

_____

_____

A Prayer

Dear Lord, when Jesus humbled Himself and became a servant,
He also became an example for me. Make me a faithful steward of
my gifts, and let me be a humble servant to my loved ones,
to my friends, and to those in need. Amen

Lesson 8

Overcoming Adversity

If you do nothing in a difficult time,
your strength is limited.
Proverbs 24:10 HCSB

THE LESSON

When tough times arrive, as they inevitably will, you should
never give in and never give up.

As life here on earth unfolds, all of us encounter occasional disappointments and setbacks: Those occasional visits from Old Man Trouble are simply a fact of life, and none of us are exempt. When tough times arrive, we may be forced to rearrange our plans and our priorities. But even on our darkest days, we must remember that God's love remains constant. And we must never forget that God intends for us to use our setbacks as stepping stones on the path to a better life.

> Take courage. We walk in the wilderness today and in the Promised Land tomorrow.
>
> —
>
> D. L. Moody

The fact that we encounter adversity is not nearly so important as the way we choose to deal with it. When tough times arrive, we have a clear choice: we can begin the difficult work of tackling our troubles . . . or not. When we summon the courage to look Old Man Trouble squarely in the eye, he usually blinks. But, if we refuse to address our problems, even the smallest annoyances have a way of growing into king-sized catastrophes.

Psalm 145 promises, "The Lord is near to all who call on him, to all who call on him in truth. He fulfills the desires of those who fear him; he hears their cry and saves them" (vv. 18-20 NIV). And the words of Jesus offer us comfort: "These things I have spoken to you, that in Me you may have peace. In the world you will have tribulation; but be of good cheer, I have overcome the world" (John 16:33 NKJV).

As believers, we know that God loves us and that He will protect us. In times of hardship, He will comfort us; in times of sorrow, He will dry our tears. When we are troubled, or weak, or sorrowful, God is always with us. We must build our lives on the rock that cannot be shaken: we must trust in God. And then, we must get on with the character-building, life-altering work of tackling our problems . . . because if we don't, who will? Or should?

SOMETHING TO THINK ABOUT

If you're having tough times, don't hit the panic button and don't keep everything bottled up inside. Talk things over with people you can really trust. A second opinion (or, for that matter, a third, fourth, or fifth opinion) is usually helpful. So if your troubles seem overwhelming, be willing to seek outside help—starting, of course, with your pastor.

Your greatest ministry will likely come out of your greatest hurt.

Rick Warren

The fear of God is the death of every other fear.

C. H. Spurgeon

God will not permit any troubles to come upon us unless He has a specific plan by which great blessing can come out of the difficulty.

Peter Marshall

Jesus does not say, "There is no storm." He says, "I am here, do not toss, but trust."

Vance Havner

As we wait on God, He helps us use the winds of adversity to soar above our problems. As the Bible says, "Those who wait on the LORD…shall mount up with wings like eagles."

Billy Graham

Have courage for the great sorrows of life and patience for the small ones; and when you have laboriously accomplished your daily task, go to sleep in peace. God is awake.

Victor Hugo

MORE FROM GOD'S WORD

God is our refuge and strength, a very present help in trouble.

Psalm 46:1 NKJV

We also rejoice in our afflictions, because we know that affliction produces endurance, endurance produces proven character, and proven character produces hope.

Romans 5:3-4 HCSB

The Lord is a refuge for the oppressed, a refuge in times of trouble.

Psalm 9:9 HCSB

For You delivered me from death, even my feet from stumbling, to walk before God in the light of life.

Psalm 56:13 HCSB

Be anxious for nothing, but in everything by prayer and supplication, with thanksgiving, let your requests be made known to God.

Philippians 4:6 NKJV

MY THOUGHTS ON THIS LESSON

A PRAYER

Heavenly Father, You are my strength and my refuge.
As I journey through this day, I know that I may encounter
disappointments and losses. When I am troubled, let me turn to
You. Keep me steady, Lord, and renew a right spirit
inside of me this day and forever. Amen

Lesson 9

Forgiveness Now

A person's insight gives him patience,
and his virtue is to overlook an offense.

Proverbs 19:11 HCSB

THE LESSON

God wants you to forgive the people who have hurt you, and
He wants you to forgive them now.

Christ understood the importance of forgiveness when he commanded, "Love your enemies and pray for those who persecute you" (Matthew 5:43-44 NIV). But sometimes, forgiveness is difficult indeed.

When we have been injured or embarrassed, we feel the urge to strike back and to hurt the ones who have hurt us. But Christ instructs us to do otherwise. Christ teaches us that forgiveness is God's way and that mercy is an integral part of God's plan for our lives. In short, we are commanded to weave the thread of forgiveness into the very fabric of our lives.

Do you invest more time than you should reliving the past? Are you troubled by feelings of anger, bitterness, envy, or regret? Do you harbor ill will against someone whom you simply can't seem to forgive? If so, it's time to finally get serious about forgiveness.

> There is always room for more loving forgiveness within our homes.
>
> —
>
> *James Dobson*

When someone hurts you, the act of forgiveness is difficult, but necessary. Until you forgive, you are trapped in a prison of your own creation. But what if you have tried to forgive and simply can't seem to do so? The solution to your dilemma is this: you simply must make forgiveness a higher priority in your life.

Most of us don't spend too much time thinking about forgiveness; we worry, instead, about the injustices we have suffered and the people who inflicted them. God has a better plan: He wants us to live in the present, not the past, and He knows that in order to do so, we must forgive those who have harmed us.

Have you made forgiveness a high priority? Have you sincerely asked God to forgive you for your inability to forgive others? Have you genuinely prayed that those feelings of hatred and anger might be swept from your heart? If so, congratulations. If not, perhaps it's time to rearrange your priorities . . . and perhaps it's time to fortify your character by freeing yourself from the chains of bitterness and regret.

SOMETHING TO THINK ABOUT

Today, make a list of the people you still need to forgive. Then make up your mind to forgive at least one person on that list. Finally, ask God to cleanse your heart of bitterness, animosity, and regret. If you ask Him sincerely and often, He will respond.

As you have received the mercy of God by the forgiveness of sin and the promise of eternal life, thus you must show mercy.

Billy Graham

To be a Christian means to forgive the inexcusable, because God has forgiven the inexcusable in you.

C. S. Lewis

Learning how to forgive and forget is one of the secrets of a happy Christian life.

Warren Wiersbe

God's heart of mercy provides for us not only pardon from sin but also a daily provision of spiritual food to strengthen us.

Jim Cymbala

Bitterness is the trap that snares the hunter.

Max Lucado

Forgiveness is the key that unlocks the door of resentment and the handcuffs of hate. It is a power that breaks the chains of bitterness and the shackles of selfishness.

Corrie ten Boom

MORE FROM GOD'S WORD

Then Peter came to Him and said, "Lord, how many times could my brother sin against me and I forgive him? As many as seven times?" "I tell you, not as many as seven," Jesus said to him, "but 70 times seven."

Matthew 18:21-22 HCSB

Therefore, God's chosen ones, holy and loved, put on heartfelt compassion, kindness, humility, gentleness, and patience, accepting one another and forgiving one another if anyone has a complaint against another. Just as the Lord has forgiven you, so also you must forgive.

Colossians 3:12-13 HCSB

And be kind and compassionate to one another, forgiving one another, just as God also forgave you in Christ.

Ephesians 4:32 HCSB

And forgive us our sins, for we ourselves also forgive everyone in debt to us. And do not bring us into temptation.

Luke 11:4 NKJV

Be merciful, just as your Father also is merciful.

Luke 6:36 HCSB

My Thoughts on This Lesson

_____

_____

_____

_____

_____

_____

_____

_____

_____

_____

A Prayer

Heavenly Father, give me a forgiving heart. When I am bitter, Your Word reminds me that forgiveness is Your commandment. Let me be Your obedient servant, Lord, and let me be a person who forgives others just as You have forgiven me. Amen

Lesson 10

Humility Strengthens Character

When pride comes, then comes dishonor,
but with the humble is wisdom.

Proverbs 11:2 NASB

THE LESSON

Pride is a sin, and it's dangerous; humility is wisdom, and it invites God's blessings.

We have heard it said on countless occasions: "He's a self-made man," or "She's a self-made woman." In truth, none of us are self-made. We all owe countless debts that we can never repay.

Our first debt, of course, is to our Father in heaven—Who has given us everything—and to His Son Who sacrificed His own life so that we might live eternally. We are also indebted to ancestors, parents, teachers, friends, spouses, family members, coworkers, fellow believers...and the list, of course, goes on.

As Christians, we have a profound reason to be humble: We have been refashioned and saved by Jesus Christ, and that salvation came not because of our own good works but because of God's grace. Thus, we are not "self-made"; we are "God-made" and "Christ-saved." How, then, can we be boastful? The answer, of course, is that, if we are honest with ourselves and with our God, we simply can't be boastful...we must, instead, be eternally grateful and exceedingly humble.

Humility is not, in most cases, a naturally-occurring human trait. Most of us, it seems, are more than willing to stick out our chests and say, "Look at me; I did that!" But in our better moments, in the quiet moments when we search the depths of our own hearts, we know better. Whatever "it" is, God did that, not us.

> Humility is not thinking less of yourself; it is thinking of yourself less.
>
> —
>
> *Rick Warren*

St. Augustine observed, "If you plan to build a tall house of virtues, you must first lay deep foundations of humility." Are you a believer who genuinely seeks to build your house of virtues on a strong foundation of humility? If so, you are wise and you are blessed. But if you've been laboring under the misconception that you're a "self-made" man or woman, it's time to face this simple fact: your blessings come from God. And He deserves the credit.

SOMETHING TO THINK ABOUT

Remember that humility leads to happiness, and pride doesn't. Max Lucado writes, "God exalts humility. When God works in our lives, helping us to become humble, he gives us a permanent joy. Humility gives us a joy that cannot be taken away." Enough said.

Jesus had a humble heart. If He abides in us, pride will never dominate our lives.

Billy Graham

A humble heart is like a magnet that draws the favor of God toward us.

Jim Cymbala

We are never stronger than the moment we admit we are weak.

Beth Moore

The great characteristic of the saint is humility.

Oswald Chambers

I can usually sense that a leading is from the Holy Spirit when it calls me to humble myself, to serve somebody, to encourage somebody, or to give something away. Very rarely will the evil one lead us to do those kind of things.

Bill Hybels

Humility is a thing which must be genuine; the imitation of it is the nearest thing in the world to pride.

C. H. Spurgeon

MORE FROM GOD'S WORD

Therefore, God's chosen ones, holy and loved, put on heartfelt compassion, kindness, humility, gentleness, and patience.

Colossians 3:12 HCSB

Clothe yourselves with humility toward one another, because God resists the proud, but gives grace to the humble.

1 Peter 5:5 HCSB

Humble yourselves therefore under the mighty hand of God, so that He may exalt you in due time, casting all your care upon Him, because He cares about you.

1 Peter 5:6-7 HCSB

But He said to me, "My grace is sufficient for you, for power is perfected in weakness." Therefore, I will most gladly boast all the more about my weaknesses, so that Christ's power may reside in me.

2 Corinthians 12:9 HCSB

You will save the humble people; but Your eyes are on the haughty, that You may bring them down.

2 Samuel 22:28 NKJV

MY THOUGHTS ON THIS LESSON

_____

_____

_____

_____

_____

_____

_____

_____

_____

A PRAYER

Heavenly Father, Jesus clothed Himself with humility when He
chose to leave heaven and come to earth to live and die for us,
His children. Christ is my Master and my example. Clothe me
with humility, Lord, so that I might be more like Your Son, and
keep me mindful that You are the giver and sustainer of life, and
to You, Dear Lord, goes the glory and the praise. Amen

Lesson 11

God Gives Us Strength

The name of the Lord is a strong tower;
the righteous run to it and are protected.

Proverbs 18:10 HCSB

THE LESSON

If you need strength, God can provide it. And, when you find strength in God, you will be protected.

It's a promise that is made over and over again in the Bible: Whatever "it" is, God can handle it.

Life isn't always easy. Far from it! Sometimes, life can seem like a long, tiring, character-building, fear-provoking journey. But even when the storm clouds form overhead, even during our darkest moments, we're protected by a loving Heavenly Father.

When we're worried, God can reassure us; when we're sad, God can comfort us. When our hearts are broken, God is not just near; He is here. So we must lift our thoughts and prayers to Him. When we do, He will answer our prayers. Why? Because He is our Shepherd, and He has promised to protect us now and forever.

God's hand uplifts those who turn their hearts and prayers to Him. Will you count yourself among that number? Will you accept God's peace and wear God's armor against the temptations and distractions of our dangerous world? If you do, you can live courageously and optimistically, knowing that even on the darkest days, you and your Heavenly Father can handle every challenge you face, today and forever.

SOMETHING TO THINK ABOUT

Today, think about ways that you can tap into God's strength: try prayer, worship, and praise, for starters.

The next time you're disappointed, don't panic. Don't give up. Just be patient and let God remind you he's still in control.

Max Lucado

The promises of God's Word sustain us in our suffering, and we know Jesus sympathizes and empathizes with us in our darkest hour.

Bill Bright

Kept by His power—that is the only safety.

Oswald Chambers

We do not understand the intricate pattern of the stars in their course, but we know that He Who created them does, and that just as surely as He guides them, He is charting a safe course for us.

Billy Graham

You may not know what you are going to do; you only know that God knows what He is going to do.

Oswald Chambers

Do not let Satan deceive you into being afraid of God's plans for your life.

R. A. Torrey

Jesus has been consistently affectionate and true to us. He has shared his great wealth with us. How can we doubt the all-powerful, all-sufficient Lord?

C. H. Spurgeon

God's saints in all ages have realized that God was enough for them. God is enough for time; God is enough for eternity. God is enough!

Hannah Whitall Smith

God will call you to obey Him and do whatever he asks of you. However, you do not need to be doing something to feel fulfilled. You are fulfilled completely in a relationship with God. When you are filled with Him, what else do you need?

Henry Blackaby and Claude King

The God we seek is a God who is intrinsically righteous and who will be so forever. With His example and His strength, we can share in that righteousness.

Bill Hybels

If not a sparrow falls upon the ground without your Father, you have reason to see that the smallest events of your career and your life are arranged by him.

C. H. Spurgeon

MORE FROM GOD'S WORD

Cast your burden on the Lord, and He will support you; He will never allow the righteous to be shaken.

Psalm 55:22 HCSB

He gives strength to the weary and strengthens the powerless.

Isaiah 40:29 HCSB

Finally, be strengthened by the Lord and by His vast strength.

Ephesians 6:10 HCSB

You, therefore, my child, be strong in the grace that is in Christ Jesus.

2 Timothy 2:1 HCSB

The Lord is my strength and my song; He has become my salvation.

Exodus 15:2 HCSB

MY THOUGHTS ON THIS LESSON

_____

_____

_____

_____

_____

_____

_____

_____

_____

A PRAYER

Dear Lord, You rule over our world, and I will allow You to rule
over my heart. I will obey Your commandments,
I will study Your Word, and I will seek Your will for my life,
today and every day of my life. Amen

Lesson 12

It Pays to Be Kind

A kind man benefits himself,
but a cruel man brings disaster on himself.
Proverbs 11:17 HCSB

THE LESSON

God wants you to be a kind and compassionate, and He will reward you when you are.

The noted American theologian Phillips Brooks advised, "Be such a man, and live such a life, that if every man were such as you, and every life a life like yours, this earth would be God's Paradise." One tangible way to make the world a more godly place is to spread kindness wherever you go.

"While we were still sinners, Christ died for us" (Romans 5:8 NIV). We, as Christ's followers, are challenged to share His love with kind words on our lips and praise in our hearts. Just as Christ has been—and will always be—the ultimate friend to His flock, so should we be Christlike in the kindness and generosity that we show toward others, especially those who are most in need.

Today, as you consider all the things that Christ has done in your life, honor Him by being a little kinder than necessary. Honor Him by slowing down long enough to say an extra word of encouragement to someone who needs it. Honor Him by picking up the phone and calling a distant friend…for no reason other than to say, "I'm thinking of you." Honor Christ by following His commandment and obeying the Golden Rule. He expects no less, and He deserves no less.

SOMETHING TO THINK ABOUT

As you plan for the day ahead, remember this: kind words cost nothing, but when they're spoken at the right time, they can be priceless.

There are many timid souls whom we jostle morning and evening as we pass them by; but if only the kind word were spoken they might become fully persuaded.

Fanny Crosby

Encouraging others means helping people, looking for the best in them, and trying to bring out their positive qualities.

John Maxwell

When you extend hospitality to others, you're not trying to impress people, you're trying to reflect God to them.

Max Lucado

If we have the true love of God in our hearts, we will show it in our lives. We will not have to go up and down the earth proclaiming it. We will show it in everything we say or do.

D. L. Moody

The mark of a Christian is that he will walk the second mile and turn the other cheek. A wise man or woman gives the extra effort, all for the glory of the Lord Jesus Christ.

John Maxwell

When you launch an act of kindness out into the crosswinds of life, it will blow kindness back to you.

Dennis Swanberg

Kindness in this world will do much to help others, not only to come into the light, but also to grow in grace day by day.

Fanny Crosby

It is one of the most beautiful compensations of life that no one can sincerely try to help another without helping herself.

Barbara Johnson

It doesn't take monumental feats to make the world a better place. It can be as simple as letting someone go ahead of you in a grocery line.

Barbara Johnson

What is your focus today? Joy comes when it is Jesus first, others second…then you.

Kay Arthur

Be so preoccupied with good will that you haven't room for ill will.

E. Stanley Jones

MORE FROM GOD'S WORD

Therefore, God's chosen ones, holy and loved, put on heartfelt compassion, kindness, humility, gentleness, and patience.

Colossians 3:12 HCSB

And be kind and compassionate to one another, forgiving one another, just as God also forgave you in Christ.

Ephesians 4:32 HCSB

Carry one another's burdens; in this way you will fulfill the law of Christ.

Galatians 6:2 HCSB

Now finally, all of you should be like-minded and sympathetic, should love believers, and be compassionate and humble.

1 Peter 3:8 HCSB

And may the Lord make you increase and abound in love to one another and to all.

1 Thessalonians 3:12 NKJV

MY THOUGHTS ON THIS LESSON

_____

_____

_____

_____

_____

_____

_____

_____

_____

_____

A PRAYER

Help me, Lord, to see the needs of those around me.
Today, let me show courtesy to those who cross my path.
Today, let me spread kind words in honor of Your Son.
Today, let forgiveness rule my heart. And every day, Lord,
let my love for Christ be demonstrated through the acts of
kindness that I offer to those who need the healing touch
of the Master's hand. Amen

Lesson 13

The Power of Perseverance

Though a righteous man falls seven times, he will get up,
but the wicked will stumble into ruin.

Proverbs 24:16 HCSB

THE LESSON

During difficult times, you may be tempted to give up. But, God's Word makes it clear that perseverance pays big dividends.

As you continue to seek God's purpose for your life, you will undoubtedly experience your fair share of disappointments, detours, false starts, and failures. When you do, don't become discouraged: God's not finished with you yet.

The old saying is as true today as it was when it was first spoken: "Life is a marathon, not a sprint." That's why wise travelers (like you) select a traveling companion who never tires and never falters. That partner, of course, is your Heavenly Father.

> Don't quit. For if you do, you may miss the answer to your prayers.
>
> —
>
> *Max Lucado*

The next time you find your courage tested to the limit, remember that God is as near as your next breath, and remember that He offers strength and comfort to His children. He is your shield and your strength; He is your protector and your deliverer. Call upon Him in your hour of need and then be comforted. Whatever your challenge, whatever your trouble, God can help you persevere. And that's precisely what He'll do if you ask Him.

Perhaps you are in a hurry for God to help you resolve your difficulties. Perhaps you're anxious to earn the rewards that you feel you've already earned from life. Perhaps you're drumming your fingers, impatiently waiting for God to act. If so, be forewarned: God operates on His own timetable, not yours. Sometimes, God may answer your prayers with silence, and when He does, you must patiently persevere. In times of trouble, you must remain steadfast and trust in the merciful goodness of your Heavenly Father. Whatever your problem, He can manage it. Your job is to keep persevering until He does.

SOMETHING TO THINK ABOUT

Are you being tested? Call upon God. God can give you the strength to persevere, and that's exactly what you should ask Him to do.

Jesus taught that perseverance is the essential element in prayer.

E. M. Bounds

It is a remarkable thing that some of the most optimistic and enthusiastic people you will meet are those who have been through intense suffering.

Warren Wiersbe

Christ can put a spring in your step and a thrill in your heart. Optimism and cheerfulness are products of knowing Christ.

Billy Graham

Perseverance is more than endurance. It is endurance combined with absolute assurance and certainty that what we are looking for is going to happen.

Oswald Chambers

Battles are won in the trenches, in the grit and grime of courageous determination; they are won day by day in the arena of life.

Charles Swindoll

By perseverance the snail reached the ark.

C. H. Spurgeon

MORE FROM GOD'S WORD

For you need endurance, so that after you have done God's will, you may receive what was promised.

Hebrews 10:36 HCSB

Do you not know that the runners in a stadium all race, but only one receives the prize? Run in such a way that you may win. Now everyone who competes exercises self-control in everything. However, they do it to receive a perishable crown, but we an imperishable one.

1 Corinthians 9:24-25 HCSB

But as for you, be strong; don't be discouraged, for your work has a reward.

2 Chronicles 15:7 HCSB

I have fought the good fight, I have finished the race, I have kept the faith.

2 Timothy 4:7 HCSB

So we must not get tired of doing good, for we will reap at the proper time if we don't give up.

Galatians 6:9 HCSB

MY THOUGHTS ON THIS LESSON

_____

_____

_____

_____

_____

_____

_____

_____

_____

_____

A PRAYER

Lord, when life is difficult, I am tempted to abandon hope in the
future. But You are my God, and I can draw strength from You.
Let me trust You, Father, in good times and in bad times.
Let me persevere—even if my soul is troubled—and let me follow
Your Son Jesus Christ this day and forever. Amen

Lesson 14

Too Friendly with the World?

He who trusts in his riches will fall,
but the righteous will flourish.

Proverbs 11:28 NASB

THE LESSON

The world's definition of success is often in conflict with God's definition of success. When in doubt, trust God.

We live in the world, but we should not worship it—yet at every turn, or so it seems, we are tempted to do otherwise. As Warren Wiersbe correctly observed, "Because the world is deceptive, it is dangerous."

The 21st-century world in which we live is a noisy, distracting place, a place that offers countless temptations and dangers. The world seems to cry, "Worship me with your time, your money, your energy, your thoughts, and your life!" But if we are wise, we won't fall prey to that temptation.

If you wish to build your character day-by-day, you must distance yourself, at least in part, from the temptations and distractions of modern-day society. But distancing yourself isn't easy, especially when so many societal forces are struggling to capture your attention, your participation, and your money.

C. S. Lewis said, "Aim at heaven and you will get earth thrown in; aim at earth and you will get neither." That's good advice. You're likely to hit what you aim at, so aim high . . . aim at heaven. When you do, you'll be strengthening your character as you improve every aspect of your life. And God will demonstrate His approval as He showers you with more spiritual blessings than you can count.

> The only ultimate disaster that can befall us,
> I have come to realize,
> is to feel ourselves to be home on earth.
>
> —
>
> *Max Lucado*

SOMETHING TO THINK ABOUT

The world makes plenty of promises that it can't keep. God, on the other hand, keeps every single one of His promises. If you dwell on the world's messages, you're setting yourself up for disaster. If you dwell on God's message, you're setting yourself up for victory.

Here's a simple test: If you can see it, it's not going to last. The things that last are the things you cannot see.

Dennis Swanberg

Grow, dear friends, but grow, I beseech you, in God's way, which is the only true way.

Hannah Whitall Smith

Our joy ends where love of the world begins.

C. H. Spurgeon

There is no hell on earth like horizontal living without God.

Charles Swindoll

Christians don't fail to live as they should because they are in the world; they fail because the world has gotten into them.

Billy Graham

Every day, I find countless opportunities to decide whether I will obey God and demonstrate my love for Him or try to please myself or the world system. God is waiting for my choices.

Bill Bright

Our fight is not against any physical enemy; it is against organizations and powers that are spiritual. We must struggle against sin all our lives, but we are assured we will win.

Corrie ten Boom

The more we stuff ourselves with material pleasures, the less we seem to appreciate life.

Barbara Johnson

A society that pursues pleasure runs the risk of raising expectations ever higher, so that true contentment always lies tantalizingly out of reach.

Philip Yancey and Paul Brand

MORE FROM GOD'S WORD

Let no one deceive himself. If anyone among you seems to be wise in this age, let him become a fool that he may become wise. For the wisdom of this world is foolishness with God. For it is written, "He catches the wise in their own craftiness."

1 Corinthians 3:18–19 NKJV

Pure and undefiled religion before our God and Father is this: to look after orphans and widows in their distress and to keep oneself unstained by the world.

James 1:27 HCSB

Now we have not received the spirit of the world, but the Spirit who is from God, in order to know what has been freely given to us by God.

1 Corinthians 2:12 HCSB

Do not love the world or the things that belong to the world. If anyone loves the world, love for the Father is not in him.

1 John 2:15 HCSB

Do not have other gods besides Me.

Exodus 20:3 HCSB

MY THOUGHTS ON THIS LESSON

_____

_____

_____

_____

_____

_____

_____

_____

_____

_____

A PRAYER

Dear Lord, when I look to the world for approval, I suffer.
But, when I look to You for approval, I am blessed. Today, Father,
help me focus less on the world and more on You. Amen

Lesson 15

Hold On to Hope

Hope deferred makes the heart sick.

Proverbs 13:12 NKJV

THE LESSON

Since all things are possible through God, we should never lose hope.

There are few sadder sights on earth than the sight of a man or woman who has lost all hope. In difficult times, hope can be elusive, but those who place their faith in God's promises need never lose it. After all, God is good; His love endures; He has promised His children the gift of eternal life. And, God keeps His promises.

Despite God's promises, despite Christ's love, and despite our countless blessings, we frail human beings can still lose hope from time to time. When we do, we need the encouragement of Christian friends, the life-changing power of prayer, and the healing truth of God's Holy Word.

If you find yourself falling into the spiritual traps of worry and discouragement, seek the healing touch of Jesus and the encouraging words of fellow Christians. If you find a friend in need, remind him or her of the peace that is found through a personal relationship with Christ. It was Christ who promised, "These things I have spoken unto you, that in me ye might have peace. In the world ye shall have tribulation: but be of good cheer; I have overcome the world" (John 16:33 KJV). This world can be a place of trials and tribulations, but as believers, we are secure. God has promised us peace, joy, and eternal life. And, of course, God keeps His promises today, tomorrow, and forever.

> Faith looks back and draws courage; hope looks ahead and keeps desire alive.
>
> —
>
> *John Eldredge*

SOMETHING TO THINK ABOUT

If you're experiencing hard times, you'll be wise to start spending more time with God. And if you do your part, God will do His part. So never be afraid to hope—or to ask—for a miracle.

The more wisdom enters our hearts, the more we will be able to trust our hearts in difficult situations.

John Eldredge

Whatever sort of tribulation we suffer, we should always remember that its purpose is to make us spurn the present and reach out to the future.

John Calvin

The hope we have in Jesus is the anchor for the soul—something sure and steadfast, preventing drifting or giving way, lowered to the depth of God's love.

Franklin Graham

Down through the centuries in times of trouble and trial, God has brought courage to the hearts of those who love Him. The Bible is filled with assurances of God's help and comfort in every kind of trouble which might cause fears to arise in the human heart. You can look ahead with promise, hope, and joy.

Billy Graham

Joy is the direct result of having God's perspective on our daily lives and the effect of loving our Lord enough to obey His commands and trust His promises.

Bill Bright

No other religion, no other philosophy promises new bodies, hearts, and minds. Only in the Gospel of Christ do hurting people find such incredible hope.

Joni Eareckson Tada

Never yield to gloomy anticipation. Place your hope and confidence in God. He has no record of failure.

Mrs. Charles E. Cowman

If your hopes are being disappointed just now, it means that they are being purified.

Oswald Chambers

MORE FROM GOD'S WORD

We have this hope—like a sure and firm anchor of the soul—that enters the inner sanctuary behind the curtain.

Hebrews 6:19 HCSB

Let us hold on to the confession of our hope without wavering, for He who promised is faithful.

Hebrews 10:23 HCSB

For in You, O Lord, I hope; You will hear, O Lord my God.

Psalm 38:15 NKJV

The Lord is good to those who wait for Him, to the person who seeks Him.

Lamentations 3:25 HCSB

Now may the God of hope fill you with all joy and peace in believing, so that you may overflow with hope by the power of the Holy Spirit.

Romans 15:13 HCSB

MY THOUGHTS ON THIS LESSON

A PRAYER

Dear Lord, if I become discouraged, let me turn to You.
If I grow weary, let me seek strength in You. When I face
adversity, let me seek Your will and trust Your Word. In every
aspect of my life, I will trust You, Father, so that my heart
will be filled with faith and hope, this day and forever. Amen

Lesson 16

The Rewards of Hard Work

Hard work means prosperity;
only fools idle away their time.

Proverbs 12:11 NLT

THE LESSON

Hard work pays; laziness costs.

The old adage is both familiar and true: We must pray as if everything depended upon God, but work as if everything depended upon us. Yet sometimes, when we are weary and discouraged, we may allow our worries to sap our energy and our hope. God has other intentions. God intends that we pray for things, and He intends that we be willing to work for the things that we pray for. More importantly, God intends that our work should become His work.

Whether you're in school or in the workplace, your success will depend, in large part, upon the passion that you bring to your work. God has created a world in which diligence is rewarded and sloth is not. So whatever you choose to do, do it with commitment, with excitement, with enthusiasm, and with vigor.

> You can't climb the ladder of life with your hands in your pockets.
>
> —
>
> *Barbara Johnson*

In his second letter to the Thessalonians, Paul warns, "if any would not work, neither should he eat" (3:10 KJV). And the Book of Proverbs proclaims, "One who is slack in his work is brother to one who destroys" (18:9 NIV). Clearly, God's Word commends the value and importance of diligence. Yet we live in a world that, all too often, glorifies leisure while downplaying the importance of shoulder-to-the wheel hard work. Rest assured, however, that God does not underestimate the value of diligence. And neither should you.

God did not create you to be ordinary; He created you for far greater things. Reaching for greater things usually requires work and lots of it, which is perfectly fine with God. After all, He knows that you're up to the task, and He has big plans for you. Very big plans.

SOMETHING TO THINK ABOUT

Here's a time-tested formula for success: have faith in God and do the work. It has been said that there are no shortcuts to any place worth going. Hard work is not simply a proven way to get ahead, it's also part of God's plan for all His children (including you).

Chiefly the mold of a man's fortune is in his own hands.

Francis Bacon

If one examines the secret behind a championship football team, a magnificent orchestra, or a successful business, the principal ingredient is invariably discipline.

James Dobson

Personal humility is a spiritual discipline and the hallmark of the service of Jesus.

Franklin Graham

Thank God every morning when you get up that you have something which must be done, whether you like it or not. Work breeds a hundred virtues that idleness never knows.

Charles Kingsley

Christians are to "labor," which refers to hard, manual work. Hard work is honorable. As Christians we should work hard so that we will have enough to give to those in need, not so that we will have more of what we don't need.

John MacArthur

MORE FROM GOD'S WORD

Do not lack diligence; be fervent in spirit; serve the Lord.

Romans 12:11 HCSB

Whatever you do, do it enthusiastically, as something done for the Lord and not for men.

Colossians 3:23 HCSB

Be strong and courageous, and do the work. Don't be afraid or discouraged, for the Lord God, my God, is with you. He won't leave you or forsake you.

1 Chronicles 28:20 HCSB

But thanks be to God, who gives us the victory through our Lord Jesus Christ. Therefore, my beloved brethren, be steadfast, immovable, always abounding in the work of the Lord, knowing that your labor is not in vain in the Lord.

1 Corinthians 15:57-58 NKJV

Now the one who plants and the one who waters are equal, and each will receive his own reward according to his own labor.

1 Corinthians 3:8 HCSB

MY THOUGHTS ON THIS LESSON

A PRAYER

Lord, let me be an industrious worker in Your fields.
Those fields are ripe, Lord, and Your workers are few.
Let me be counted as Your faithful, diligent servant today,
and every day. Amen

Lesson 17

Putting God First

*So you may walk in the way of goodness,
and keep to the paths of righteousness.
For the upright will dwell in the land,
and the blameless will remain in it.*

Proverbs 2:20-21 NKJV

THE LESSON

When you live righteously and put God first, you will be blessed.

One of the quickest ways to build a better life—perhaps the only way—is to do it with God as your partner. So here's a question worth thinking about: Have you made God your top priority by offering Him your heart, your soul, your talents, and your time? Or are you in the habit of giving God little more than a few hours on Sunday morning? The answer to these questions will determine, to a surprising extent, the direction of your day and your life.

As you contemplate your own relationship with God, remember this: all of mankind is engaged in the practice of worship. Some folks choose to worship God and, as a result, reap the joy that He intends for His children to experience. Other folks, folks who are stubbornly determined to do it "their way," distance themselves from God by worshiping such things as earthly possessions or personal gratification . . . and when they do, they suffer.

> When all else is gone,
> God is still left.
> Nothing changes Him.
>
> —
>
> *Hannah Whitall Smith*

In the book of Exodus, God warns that we should place no gods before Him (20:3). Yet all too often, we place our Lord in second, third, or fourth place as we worship the gods of pride, greed, power, or lust.

Does God rule your heart? Make certain that the honest answer to this question is a resounding yes. If you sincerely wish to build your life on an unshakable foundation, you must put your Creator in first place. No exceptions.

SOMETHING TO THINK ABOUT

Think about your priorities. Are you really putting God first in your life, or are you putting other things—things like possessions, pleasures, or personal status—ahead of your relationship with the Father. And if your priorities for life are misaligned, think of at least three things you can do today to put God where He belongs: in first place.

We become whatever we are committed to.

Rick Warren

A disciple is a follower of Christ. That means you take on His priorities as your own. His agenda becomes your agenda. His mission becomes your mission.

Charles Stanley

Imagine the spiritual strength the disciples drew from walking hundreds of miles with Jesus . . . (3 John 4).

Jim Maxwell

God calls us to be committed to Him, to be committed to making a difference, and to be committed to reconciliation.

Bill Hybels

Christ is not valued at all unless He is valued above all.

St. Augustine

To God be the glory, great things He has done; / So loved He the world that He gave us His Son.

Fanny Crosby

One with God is a majority.

Billy Graham

Jesus Christ is the first and last, author and finisher, beginning and end, alpha and omega, and by Him all other things hold together. He must be first or nothing. God never comes next!

Vance Havner

It is God to whom and with whom we travel, and while He is the End of our journey, He is also at every stopping place.

Elisabeth Elliot

MORE FROM GOD'S WORD

But seek first the kingdom of God and His righteousness, and all these things will be provided for you.

Matthew 6:33 HCSB

No one has ever seen God. If we love one another, God remains in us and His love is perfected in us.

1 John 4:12 HCSB

He that loveth not, knoweth not God; for God is love.

1 John 4:8 KJV

You shall have no other gods before Me.

Exodus 20:3 NKJV

Yet Lord, You are our Father; we are the clay, and You are our potter; we all are the work of Your hands.

Isaiah 64:8 HCSB

My Thoughts on This Lesson

_____

_____

_____

_____

_____

_____

_____

_____

_____

A Prayer

Dear Lord, today I will honor You with my thoughts, my actions,
and my prayers. I will seek to please You, and I will strive to serve
You. Your blessings are as limitless as Your love. And because
I have been so richly blessed, I will worship You, Father,
with thanksgiving in my heart and praise on my lips,
this day and forever. Amen

Lesson 18

The Right Kind
of Attitude

A cheerful heart has a continual feast.
Proverbs 15:15 HCSB

THE LESSON

Cheerfulness is its own reward, but not its only reward.

Of course you've heard the saying, "Life is what you make it." And although that statement may seem very trite, it's also very true. You can choose a life filled to the brim with frustration and fear, or you can choose a life of abundance and peace. That choice is up to you—and only you—and it depends, to a surprising extent, upon your attitude.

What's your attitude today? Are you fearful, angry, bored, or worried? Are you pessimistic, perplexed, pained, and perturbed? Are you moping around with a frown on your face that's almost as big as the one in your heart? If so, God wants to have a little talk with you.

God created you in His own image, and He wants you to experience joy, contentment, peace, and abundance. But, God will not force you to experience these things; you must claim them for yourself.

God has given you free will, including the ability to influence the direction and the tone of your thoughts. And, here's how God wants you to direct those thoughts:

Finally brothers, whatever is true, whatever is honorable, whatever is just, whatever is pure, whatever is lovely, whatever is commendable—if there is any moral excellence and if there is any praise—dwell on these things (Philippians 4:8 HCSB).

The quality of your attitude will help determine the quality of your life, so you must guard your thoughts accordingly. If you make up your mind to approach life with a healthy mixture of realism and optimism, you'll be rewarded. But, if you allow yourself to fall into the unfortunate habit of negative thinking, you will doom yourself to unhappiness, or mediocrity, or worse.

So, the next time you find yourself dwelling upon the negative aspects of your life, refocus your attention on things positive. The next time you find yourself falling prey to the blight of pessimism, stop yourself and turn your thoughts around. The next time you're tempted to waste valuable time gossiping or complaining, resist those temptations with all your might.

And remember this important tip: You'll never whine your way to the top . . . so don't waste your breath.

SOMETHING TO THINK ABOUT

Today, create a positive attitude by focusing on opportunities, not roadblocks. Of course you may have experienced disappointments in the past, and you will undoubtedly experience some setbacks in the future. But don't invest large amounts of energy focusing on past misfortunes. Instead, look to the future with optimism and hope.

The people whom I have seen succeed best in life have always been cheerful and hopeful people who went about their business with a smile on their faces.

Charles Kingsley

People who inspire others are those who see invisible bridges at the end of dead-end streets.

Charles Swindoll

God is always far more willing to give us good things than we are anxious to have them.

Catherine Marshall

The essence of optimism is that it takes no account of the present, but it is a source of inspiration, of vitality, and of hope. Where others have resigned, it enables a man to hold his head high, to claim the future for himself, and not abandon it to his enemy.

Dietrich Bonhoeffer

Keep your feet on the ground, but let your heart soar as high as it will. Refuse to be average or to surrender to the chill of your spiritual environment.

A. W. Tozer

MORE FROM GOD'S WORD

Your attitude should be the same as that of Christ Jesus: Who, being in very nature God, did not consider equality with God something to be grasped, but made himself nothing, taking the very nature of a servant, being made in human likeness. And being found in appearance as a man, he humbled himself and became obedient to death—even death on a cross!

Philippians 2:5-8 NIV

The Lord values those who fear Him, those who put their hope in His faithful love.

Psalm 147:11 HCSB

For the word of God is living and powerful, and sharper than any two-edged sword, piercing even to the division of soul and spirit, and of joints and marrow, and is a discerner of the thoughts and intents of the heart.

Hebrews 4:12 NKJV

Set your minds on what is above, not on what is on the earth.

Colossians 3:2 HCSB

MY THOUGHTS ON THIS LESSON

_____

_____

_____

_____

_____

_____

_____

_____

_____

A PRAYER

Lord, let me be an expectant Christian. Let me expect the best from You, and let me look for the best in others. If I become discouraged, Father, turn my thoughts and my prayers to You. Let me trust You, Lord, to direct my life. And, let me share my faith and optimism with others, today and every day that I live. Amen

Lesson 19

Simplicity Now

Better a little with the fear of the Lord
than great treasure with turmoil.
Proverbs 15:16 HCSB

THE LESSON

Simplicity pays; complexity costs; live accordingly.

You live in a world where simplicity is in short supply. Think for a moment about the complexity of your everyday life and compare it to the lives of your ancestors. Certainly, you are the beneficiary of many technological innovations, but those innovations have a price: in all likelihood, your world is highly complex. Consider the following:

1. From the moment you wake up in the morning until the time you lay your head on the pillow at night, you are the target of an endless stream of advertising information. Each message is intended to grab your attention in order to convince you to purchase things you didn't know you needed (and probably don't!).

2. Essential aspects of your life, including personal matters such as healthcare, are subject to an ever-increasing flood of rules and regulations.

3. Unless you take firm control of your time and your life, you may be overwhelmed by an ever-increasing tidal wave of complexity that threatens your happiness.

Your Heavenly Father understands the joy of living simply, and so should you. So do yourself a favor: keep your life as simple as possible. Simplicity is, indeed, genius. By simplifying your life, you are destined to improve it.

SOMETHING TO THINK ABOUT

Simplicity and peace are two concepts that are closely related. Complexity and peace are not.

All that a Christian does, even in eating and sleeping, is prayer, when it is done in simplicity, according to the order of God, without either adding to or diminishing from it by His choice.

John Wesley

We often become mentally and spiritually barren because we're so busy.

Franklin Graham

Frustration is not the will of God. There is time to do anything and everything that God wants us to do.

Elisabeth Elliot

There is absolutely no evidence that complexity and materialism lead to happiness. On the contrary, there is plenty of evidence that simplicity and spirituality lead to joy, a blessedness that is better than happiness.

Dennis Swanberg

The most powerful life is the most simple life. The most powerful life is the life that knows where it's going, that knows where the source of strength is; it is the life that stays free of clutter and happenstance and hurriedness.

Max Lucado

It is part of Satan's program to make our faith complicated and involved. Now and then, we need a rediscovery of the simplicity that is in Christ and in our faith in Him.

Vance Havner

Daily Bible reading is essential to victorious living and real Christian growth.

Billy Graham

The foe of opportunity is preoccupation. Just when God sends along a chance to turn a great victory for mankind, some of us are too busy puttering around to notice it.

A. W. Tozer

God wants to revolutionize our lives—by showing us how knowing Him can be the most powerful force to help us become all we want to be.

Bill Hybels

Nobody is going to simplify your life for you. You've got to simplify things for yourself.

Marie T. Freeman

MORE FROM GOD'S WORD

But godliness with contentment is a great gain. For we brought nothing into the world, and we can take nothing out. But if we have food and clothing, we will be content with these. But those who want to be rich fall into temptation, a trap, and many foolish and harmful desires, which plunge people into ruin and destruction.

1 Timothy 6:6-9 HCSB

"I made all this! I own all this!" God's Decree. "But there is something I'm looking for: a person simple and plain, reverently responsive to what I say."

Isaiah 66:2 MSG

Your life should be free from the love of money. Be satisfied with what you have, for He Himself has said, I will never leave you or forsake you.

Hebrews 13:5 HCSB

Do you not know that friendship with the world is hostility toward God? So whoever wants to be the world's friend becomes God's enemy.

James 4:4 HCSB

MY THOUGHTS ON THIS LESSON

_____

_____

_____

_____

_____

_____

_____

_____

_____

A PRAYER

Dear Lord, help me understand the joys of simplicity.
Life is complicated enough without my adding to the confusion.
Wherever I happen to be, help me to keep it simple—
very simple. Amen

Lesson 20

Forming the Right Kind of Habits

Guard your heart above all else,
for it is the source of life.

Proverbs 4:23 HCSB

THE LESSON

God wants you to guard your heart against destructive thoughts and destructive habits.

It's an old saying and a true one: First, you make your habits, and then your habits make you. Some habits are character-builders, inevitably bringing you closer to God while other habits will lead you away from the path He has chosen for you. If you sincerely desire to improve your spiritual health, you must honestly examine the habits that make up the fabric of your day. And you must abandon those habits that are displeasing to God.

Perhaps you've tried to become a more disciplined person, but you're still falling back into your old habits. If so, don't get discouraged. Instead, you should become even more determined to evolve into the person God wants you to be.

If you trust God, and if you keep asking for His help, He can transform your life. If you sincerely ask Him to help you, the same God who created the universe will help you defeat the harmful habits that have heretofore defeated you. So, if at first you don't succeed, keep praying. God is listening, and He's ready to help you become a better person if you ask Him . . . so ask today.

SOMETHING TO THINK ABOUT

Target your most unhealthy habit first, and attack it with vigor. When it comes to defeating harmful habitual behaviors, you'll need focus, determination, more focus, and more determination.

You will never change your life until you change something you do daily.

John Maxwell

Although our actions have nothing to do with gaining our own salvation, they might be used by God to save somebody else! What we do really matters, and it can affect the eternities of people we care about.

Bill Hybels

The alternative to discipline is disaster.

Vance Havner

The simple fact is that if we sow a lifestyle that is in direct disobedience to God's reveled Word, we ultimately reap disaster.

Charles Swindoll

Since behaviors become habits, make them work with you and not against you.

E. Stanley Jones

Begin to be now what you will be hereafter.

St. Jerome

Since behaviors become habits, make them work with you and not against you.

E. Stanley Jones

Prayer is a habit. Worship is a habit. Kindness is a habit. And if you want to please God, you'd better make sure that these habits are your habits.

Marie T. Freeman

He who does not overcome small faults, shall fall little by little into greater ones.

Thomas à Kempis

You can build up a set of good habits so that you habitually take the Christian way without thought.

E. Stanley Jones

We are always making an offering. If we do not give to God, we give to the devil.

Vance Havner

MORE FROM GOD'S WORD

Do not be deceived: "Evil company corrupts good habits."

1 Corinthians 15:33 NKJV

Dear friend, I pray that you may prosper in every way and be in good health, just as your soul prospers.

3 John 1:2 HCSB

Therefore, brothers, by the mercies of God, I urge you to present your bodies as a living sacrifice, holy and pleasing to God; this is your spiritual worship.

Romans 12:1 HCSB

Don't you know that you are God's sanctuary and that the Spirit of God lives in you?

1 Corinthians 3:16 HCSB

Do you not know that your body is a sanctuary of the Holy Spirit who is in you, whom you have from God? You are not your own, for you were bought at a price; therefore glorify God in your body.

1 Corinthians 6:19-20 HCSB

MY THOUGHTS ON THIS LESSON

A PRAYER

Dear Lord, help me break bad habits and form good ones.
And let my actions be pleasing to You,
today and every day. Amen

Lesson 21

Beyond Envy

A tranquil heart is life to the body,
but jealousy is rottenness to the bones.

Proverbs 14:30 HCSB

THE LESSON

Envy is a sin that makes you dissatisfied, discouraged, and unhappy. So, don't be envious.

Because we are frail, imperfect human beings, we are sometimes envious of others. But God's Word warns us that envy is sin. Thus, we must guard ourselves against the natural tendency to feel resentment and jealousy when other people experience good fortune.

As believers, we have absolutely no reason to be envious of any people on earth. After all, as Christians we are already recipients of the greatest gift in all creation: God's grace. We have been promised the gift of eternal life through God's only begotten Son, and we must count that gift as our most precious possession.

Rather than succumbing to the sin of envy, we should focus on the marvelous things that God has done for us—starting with Christ's sacrifice. And we must refrain from preoccupying ourselves with the blessings that God has chosen to give others.

So here's a surefire formula for a happier, healthier life: Count your own blessings and let your neighbors count theirs. It's the godly way to live.

SOMETHING TO THINK ABOUT

Envy is a sin, that robs you of contentment and peace. So you must refuse to let feelings of envy invade your thoughts or your heart.

It is the thoughts and intents of the heart that shape a person's life.

John Eldredge

I became aware of one very important concept I had missed before: my attitude—not my circumstances—was what was making me unhappy.

Vonette Bright

When you worry about what you don't have, you won't be able to enjoy what you do have.

Charles Swindoll

As a moth gnaws a garment, so does envy consume a man.

St. John Chrysostom

What God asks, does, or requires of others is not my business; it is His.

Kay Arthur

Contentment comes when we develop an attitude of gratitude for the important things we do have in our lives that we tend to take for granted if we have our eyes staring longingly at our neighbor's stuff.

Dave Ramsey

Too many Christians envy the sinners their pleasure and the saints their joy because they don't have either one.

Martin Luther

Discontent dries up the soul.

Elisabeth Elliot

When you envy your neighbor, you give demons a place to rest.

Ephraem the Syrian

Every major spiritual battle is in the mind.

Charles Stanley

How can you possess the miseries of envy when you possess in Christ the best of all portions?

C. H. Spurgeon

MORE FROM GOD'S WORD

Do not covet your neighbor's house . . . or anything that belongs to your neighbor.

Exodus 20:17 HCSB

Stop your anger! Turn from your rage! Do not envy others—it only leads to harm.

Psalm 37:8 NLT

We must not become conceited, provoking one another, envying one another.

Galatians 5:26 HCSB

If your sinful nature controls your mind, there is death. But if the Holy Spirit controls your mind, there is life and peace.

Romans 8:6 NLT

I have told you these things, so that in me you may have peace. In this world you will have trouble. But take heart! I have overcome the world.

John 16:33 NIV

MY THOUGHTS ON THIS LESSON

_____

_____

_____

_____

_____

_____

_____

_____

_____

_____

A PRAYER

Dear Lord, when I am envious of others, change my thoughts
and guard my heart. Make me a thankful Christian, Father,
and deliver me from envy. Amen

Lesson 22

Acknowledging His Presence

The eyes of the Lord are everywhere,
keeping watch on the wicked and the good.

Proverbs 15:3 NIV

THE LESSON

God isn't far away—He's right here, right now. And He's willing to talk to you right here, right now.

In the quiet early morning, as the sun's first rays peak over the horizon, we may sense the presence of God. But as the day wears on and the demands of everyday life bear down upon us, we may become so wrapped up in earthly concerns that we forget to praise the Creator.

God is everywhere we have ever been and everywhere we will ever be. When we turn to Him often, we are blessed by His presence. But, if we ignore God's presence or rebel against it altogether, the world in which we live soon becomes a spiritual wasteland.

> Whatever hallway you're in—no matter how long, how dark, or how scary—God is right there with you.
>
> —
>
> *Bill Hybels*

Since God is everywhere, we are free to sense His presence whenever we take the time to quiet our souls and turn our prayers to Him. But sometimes, amid the incessant demands of everyday life, we turn our thoughts far from God; when we do, we suffer.

Are you tired, discouraged, or fearful? Be comforted because God is with you. Are you confused? Listen to the quiet voice of your Heavenly Father. Are you bitter? Talk with God and seek His guidance. Are you celebrating a great victory? Thank God and praise Him. He is the Giver of all things good. In whatever condition you find yourself—whether you are happy or sad, victorious or vanquished, troubled or triumphant—celebrate God's presence. And be comforted in the knowledge that God is not just near. He is here.

SOMETHING TO THINK ABOUT

Having trouble hearing God? If so, slow yourself down, tune out the distractions, and listen carefully. God has important things to say; your task is to be still and listen.

There is a basic urge: the longing for unity. You desire a reunion with God—with God your Father.

E. Stanley Jones

The love of God is so vast, the power of his touch so invigorating, we could just stay in his presence for hours, soaking up his glory, basking in His blessings.

Debra Evans

It is God to whom and with whom we travel, and while He is the End of our journey, He is also at every stopping place.

Elisabeth Elliot

No matter what trials we face, Christ never leaves us.

Billy Graham

The next time you hear a baby laugh or see an ocean wave, take note. Pause and listen as his Majesty whispers ever so gently, "I'm here."

Max Lucado

The real test of being in the presence of God is that you either forget about yourself altogether or see yourself as a very small object. It is better to forget about yourself altogether.

C. S. Lewis

Get yourself into the presence of the loving Father. Just place yourself before Him, and look up into, His face; think of His love, His wonderful, tender, pitying love.

Andrew Murray

Give yourself a gift today: be present with yourself. God is. Enjoy your own personality. God does.

Barbara Johnson

Even when we cannot see the why and wherefore of God's dealings, we know that there is love in and behind them, so we can rejoice always.

J. I. Packer

More from God's Word

Draw near to God, and He will draw near to you.

James 4:8 HCSB

Now he who keeps His commandments abides in Him, and He in him. And by this we know that He abides in us, by the Spirit whom He has given us.

1 John 3:24 NKJV

For the eyes of the Lord range throughout the earth to show Himself strong for those whose hearts are completely His.

2 Chronicles 16:9 HCSB

From one man He has made every nation of men to live all over the earth and has determined their appointed times and the boundaries of where they live, so that they might seek God, and perhaps they might reach out and find Him, though He is not far from each one of us.

Acts 17:26-27 HCSB

You will seek Me and find Me when you search for Me with all your heart.

Jeremiah 29:13 HCSB

MY THOUGHTS ON THIS LESSON

_____

_____

_____

_____

_____

_____

_____

_____

_____

_____

A PRAYER

Dear Lord, You are with me always. Help me feel
Your presence in every situation and every circumstance.
Today, Dear God, let me feel You and acknowledge
Your presence, Your love, and Your Son. Amen

Lesson 23

You and Your Conscience

Souls who follow their hearts thrive;
fools bent on evil despise matters of soul.

Proverbs 13:19 MSG

THE LESSON

God has given you a conscience, and He wants you to use it.

Billy Graham correctly observed, "Most of us follow our conscience as we follow a wheelbarrow. We push it in front of us in the direction we want to go." To do so, of course, is a profound mistake. Yet all of us, on occasion, have failed to listen to the voice that God planted in our hearts, and all of us have suffered the consequences of our choices.

God gave each of us a conscience for a very good reason: to listen to it. Wise believers make it a practice to listen carefully to that quiet internal voice. Count yourself among that number. When your conscience speaks, listen and learn. In all likelihood, God is trying to get His message through. And in all likelihood, it is a message that you desperately need to hear.

Few things in life torment us more than a guilty conscience. And, few things in life provide more contentment than the knowledge that we are obeying God's commandments. A clear conscience is one of the rewards we earn when we obey God's Word and follow His will. When we follow God's will and accept His gift of salvation, our earthly rewards are never-ceasing, and our heavenly rewards are everlasting.

SOMETHING TO THINK ABOUT

Today, remember this: the more important the decision . . . the more carefully you should listen to your conscience.

To go against one's conscience is neither safe nor right. Here I stand. I cannot do otherwise.

Martin Luther

All true knowledge of God is born out of obedience.

John Calvin

The convicting work of the Holy Spirit awakens, disturbs, and judges.

Franklin Graham

He that loses his conscience has nothing left that is worth keeping.

Izaak Walton

Guilt is a healthy regret for telling God one thing and doing another.

Max Lucado

God considers a pure conscience a very valuable thing—one that keeps our faith on a steady course.

Charles Stanley

A man who gives in to temptation after five minutes simply does not know what it would have been like an hour later.

C. S. Lewis

A quiet conscience sleeps in thunder.

Thomas Fuller

Believe and do what God says. The life-changing consequences will be limitless, and the results will be confidence and peace of mind.

Franklin Graham

Let me tell you—there is no "high" like the elation and joy that come from a sacrificial act of obedience.

Bill Hybels

Obedience that is not motivated by love cannot produce the spiritual fruit that God wants from His children.

Warren Wiersbe

Obedience is the outward expression of your love of God.

Henry Blackaby

MORE FROM GOD'S WORD

Blessed is the man who does not condemn himself.

Romans 14:22 HCSB

Now the goal of our instruction is love from a pure heart, a good conscience, and a sincere faith.

1 Timothy 1:5 HCSB

If then you were raised with Christ, seek those things which are above, where Christ is, sitting at the right hand of God. Set your mind on things above, not on things on the earth.

Colossians 3:1-2 NKJV

And do not be conformed to this world, but be transformed by the renewing of your mind, that you may prove what is that good and acceptable and perfect will of God.

Romans 12:2 NKJV

For indeed, the kingdom of God is within you.

Luke 17:21 NKJV

MY THOUGHTS ON THIS LESSON

A PRAYER

Dear Lord, You speak to me through the gift of Your Holy Word.
And, Father, You speak to me through that still small voice that
tells me right from wrong. Let me follow Your way, Lord,
and, in these quiet moments, show me Your plan for this day,
that I might serve You. Amen

Lesson 24

The Importance of Prayer

The Lord is far from the wicked but he hears
the prayer of the righteous.

Proverbs 15:29 NIV

THE LESSON

There's no corner of your life that's too unimportant to pray about, so pray about everything.

In the battle to lead a righteous life, prayer is an indispensable weapon. Your life is not a destination; it is a journey that unfolds day by day. And, that's exactly how often you should seek direction from your Creator: one day at a time, each day followed by the next, without exception.

Daily prayer and meditation is a matter of will and habit. You must willingly organize your time by carving out quiet moments with God, and you must form the habit of daily worship. When you do, you'll discover that no time is more precious than the silent moments you spend with your Heavenly Father.

God promises that the prayers of righteous men and women can accomplish great things. God promises that He answers prayer (although His answers are not always in accordance with our desires). God invites us to be still and to feel His presence. So pray. Start praying before the sun comes up and keep praying until you fall off to sleep at night. Pray about matters great and small; and be watchful for the answers that God most assuredly sends your way.

> Prayer connects us with God's limitless potential.
>
> —
>
> *Henry Blackaby*

Is prayer an integral part of your daily life, or is it a hit-or-miss routine? Do you "pray without ceasing," or is your prayer life an afterthought? Do you regularly pray in the solitude of the early morning darkness, or do you bow your head only when others are watching?

The quality of your spiritual life will be in direct proportion to the quality of your prayer life. Prayer changes things, and it changes you. Today, instead of turning things over in your mind, turn them over to God in prayer. Instead of worrying about your next decision, ask God to lead the way. Don't limit your prayers to meals or to bedtime; pray constantly. God is listening; He wants to hear from you; and you most certainly need to hear from Him.

SOMETHING TO THINK ABOUT

Prayer strengthens your character and your relationship with God . . . so pray. Martin Luther observed, "If I should neglect prayer but a single day, I should lose a great deal of the fire of faith." Those words apply to you, too. And it's up to you to live—and to pray—accordingly.

When there is a matter that requires definite prayer, pray until you believe God and until you can thank Him for His answer.

Hannah Whitall Smith

What God gives in answer to our prayers will always be the thing we most urgently need, and it will always be sufficient.

Elisabeth Elliot

Prayer is not a work that can be allocated to one or another group in the church. It is everybody's responsibility; it is everybody's privilege.

A. W. Tozer

God wants to remind us that nothing on earth or in hell can ultimately stand against the man or the woman who calls on the name of the Lord!

Jim Cymbala

God shapes the world by prayer. The more praying there is in the world, the better the world will be, and the mightier will be the forces against evil.

E. M. Bounds

More from God's Word

And everything—whatever you ask in prayer, believing—you will receive.

Matthew 21:22 HCSB

The intense prayer of the righteous is very powerful.

James 5:16 HCSB

Let the words of my mouth and the meditation of my heart be acceptable in Your sight, O Lord, my strength and my Redeemer.

Psalm 19:14 NKJV

Yet He often withdrew to deserted places and prayed.

Luke 5:16 HCSB

Don't worry about anything, but in everything, through prayer and petition with thanksgiving, let your requests be made known to God.

Philippians 4:6 HCSB

MY THOUGHTS ON THIS LESSON

_____

_____

_____

_____

_____

_____

_____

_____

_____

_____

A PRAYER

Dear Lord, I will open my heart to You. I will take my concerns,
my fears, my plans, and my hopes to You in prayer.
And, then, I will trust the answers that You give. You are
my loving Father, and I will accept Your will for my life
today and every day that I live. Amen

Lesson 25

What Is Your Focus?

Let your eyes look forward;
fix your gaze straight ahead.
Proverbs 4:25 HCSB

THE LESSON

First focus on God . . . and then everything else will come
into focus.

The condition of your character is determined, to a surprising extent, by the direction of your thoughts. If you focus your thoughts and energies on matters that honor your God, your family, and yourself, you will reap rich rewards. But if you focus too intently on the distractions and temptations of our 21st-century world, you're inviting large quantities of trouble.

What is your focus today? Are you willing to focus your thoughts and energies on God's blessings and upon His will for your life? Or will you turn your thoughts to other things? Before you answer that question, consider this: God created you in His own image, and He wants you to experience joy and abundance. But, God will not force His joy upon you; you must claim it for yourself.

> Measure the size of the obstacles against the size of God.
>
> —
>
> *Beth Moore*

Today, why not focus your thoughts on the joy that is rightfully yours in Christ? Why not take time to celebrate God's glorious creation? Why not trust your hopes instead of your fears? And why not focus on God's priorities, not on the world's priorities? When you do, you'll experience the peace and the power that accrues to those who put Jesus first in their lives.

Is Christ really the focus of your life? Are you fired with enthusiasm for Him? Are you an energized Christian who allows God's Son to reign over every aspect of your day? Make no mistake: that's exactly what God intends for you to do.

God has given you the gift of eternal life through His Son. In response to God's priceless gift, you are instructed to focus your thoughts, your prayers, and your energies upon God and His only begotten Son. To do so, you must resist the subtle yet powerful temptation to become a "spiritual dabbler."

A person who dabbles in the Christian faith is unwilling to place God in His rightful place: above all other things. Resist that temptation; make God the cornerstone and the touchstone of your life. When you do, He will give you all the strength and wisdom you need to live victoriously for Him.

SOMETHING TO THINK ABOUT

Ask yourself if you're truly focusing your thoughts and energies on matters that are pleasing to God and beneficial to your family. Then ask your Creator to help you focus on His love, His Son, and His plan for your life.

As long as Jesus is one of many options, he is no option.

Max Lucado

We need to stop focusing on our lacks and stop giving out excuses and start looking at and listening to Jesus.

Anne Graham Lotz

Only the man who follows the command of Jesus single-mindedly and unresistingly let his yoke rest upon him, finds his burden easy, and under its gentle pressure receives the power to persevere in the right way.

Dietrich Bonhoeffer

If the glories of heaven were more real to us, if we lived less for material things and more for things eternal and spiritual, we would be less easily disturbed in this present life.

Billy Graham

Just like commercial organizations need to get their focus off themselves, we as individual Christians and collective churches need to recalibrate our sights on the target God has given us: spiritually lost people.

Bill Hybels

MORE FROM GOD'S WORD

Give your entire attention to what God is doing right now, and don't get worked up about what may or may not happen tomorrow. God will help you deal with whatever hard things come up when the time comes.

Matthew 6:34 MSG

Let us lay aside every weight and the sin that so easily ensnares us, and run with endurance the race that lies before us, keeping our eyes on Jesus, the source and perfecter of our faith.

Hebrews 12:1-2 HCSB

Therefore don't worry about tomorrow, because tomorrow will worry about itself. Each day has enough trouble of its own.

Matthew 6:34 HCSB

In any case, we should live up to whatever truth we have attained.

Philippians 3:16 HCSB

Enter through the narrow gate; because the gate is wide and the road is broad that leads to destruction, and there are many who go through it. How narrow is the gate and difficult the road that leads to life; and few find it.

Matthew 7:13-14 HCSB

My Thoughts on This Lesson

_____

_____

_____

_____

_____

_____

_____

_____

_____

_____

A Prayer

Dear Lord, help me to face this day with a spirit of optimism
and thanksgiving. And let me focus my thoughts on You
and Your incomparable gifts. Amen

Lesson 26

A Regular Daily Devotional Builds Character

Happy is the man who finds wisdom,
and the man who gains understanding.
Proverbs 3:13 NKJV

THE LESSON

When you find wisdom, you'll be rewarded. And, the best way to find wisdom is to seek it every day, starting with your morning devotional.

D o you have a standing appointment with God every morning? Is God your first priority, or do you talk with Him less frequently than that? If you're wise, you'll talk to God first thing every day, without exception.

Warren Wiersbe writes, "Surrender your mind to the Lord at the beginning of each day." And that's sound advice. When you begin each day with your head bowed and your heart lifted, you are reminded of God's love, His protection, and His commandments.

Then, you can align your priorities for the coming day with the teachings and commandments that God has placed upon your heart.

> Meditating upon
> His Word will inevitably
> bring peace of mind,
> strength of purpose,
> and power for living.
>
> —
>
> *Bill Bright*

Each day has 1,440 minutes— can you give God a few of them? Of course you can . . . and of course you should. So if you've acquired the unfortunate habit of trying to "squeeze" God into the corners of your life, it's time to reshuffle the items on your to-do list by placing God first. And if you haven't already done so, form the habit of spending quality time each morning with your Creator. He deserves it . . . and so, for that matter, do you.

Something to Think about

Get reacquainted with God every day. Would you like a foolproof formula for a better life? Here it is: stay in close contact with God. Hannah Whitall Smith wrote, "The crucial question for each of us is this: What do you think of Jesus, and do you yet have a personal acquaintance with Him?" Think about your relationship with Jesus: what it is and what it could be.

We must appropriate the tender mercy of God every day after conversion or problems quickly develop. We need his grace daily in order to live a righteous life.

Jim Cymbala

The vigor of our spiritual lives will be in exact proportion to the place held by the Bible in our lives and in our thoughts.

George Mueller

Either God's Word keeps you from sin, or sin keeps you from God's Word.

Corrie ten Boom

A person with no devotional life generally struggles with faith and obedience.

Charles Stanley

I suggest you discipline yourself to spend time daily in a systematic reading of God's Word. Make this "quiet time" a priority that nobody can change.

Warren Wiersbe

A child of God should never leave his bedroom in the morning without being on good terms with God.

C. H. Spurgeon

The moment you wake up each morning, all your wishes and hopes for the day rush at you like wild animals. And the first job each morning consists in shoving it all back; in listening to that other voice, taking that other point of view, letting that other, larger, stronger, quieter life coming flowing in.

C. S. Lewis

Walking in faith brings you to the Word of God. There you will be healed, cleansed, fed, nurtured, equipped, and matured.

Kay Arthur

MORE FROM GOD'S WORD

He awakens Me morning by morning, He awakens My ear to hear as the learned. The Lord God has opened My ear.

Isaiah 50:4-5 NKJV

Lord, You are my lamp; the Lord illuminates my darkness.

2 Samuel 22:29 HCSB

Teach me Your way, Lord, and I will live by Your truth. Give me an undivided mind to fear Your name.

Psalm 86:11 HCSB

I will instruct you and show you the way to go; with My eye on you, I will give counsel.

Psalm 32:8 HCSB

Yet Lord, You are our Father; we are the clay, and You are our potter; we all are the work of Your hands.

Isaiah 64:8 HCSB

MY THOUGHTS ON THIS LESSON

_____

_____

_____

_____

_____

_____

_____

_____

_____

A PRAYER

Lord, help me to hear Your direction for my life
in the quiet moments when I study Your Holy Word.
And as I go about my daily activities, let everything that I say
and do be pleasing to You. Amen

Lesson 27

The Power of Patience

Patience is better than power, and controlling one's temper, than capturing a city.
Proverbs 16:32 HCSB

THE LESSON

When tackling the inevitable challenges of everyday life, it pays to be patient.

For most of us, patience is a hard thing to master. Why? Because we have lots of things we want, and we know precisely when we want them: NOW (if not sooner). But our Father in heaven has other ideas; the Bible teaches that we must learn to wait patiently for the things that God has in store for us, even when waiting is difficult.

We live in an imperfect world inhabited by imperfect people. Sometimes, we inherit troubles from others, and sometimes we create troubles for ourselves. On other occasions, we see other people "moving ahead" in the world, and we want to move ahead with them. So we become impatient with ourselves, with our circumstances, and even with our Creator.

> You can't step in front of God and not get in trouble. When He says, "Go three steps," don't go four.
>
> —
>
> *Charles Stanley*

Psalm 37:7 commands us to "rest in the Lord, and wait patiently for Him" (NKJV). But, for most of us, waiting patiently for Him is hard. We are fallible human beings who seek solutions to our problems today, not tomorrow. Still, God instructs us to wait patiently for His plans to unfold, and that's exactly what we should do.

Sometimes, patience is the price we pay for being responsible adults, and that's as it should be. After all, think how patient our heavenly Father has been with us. So the next time you find yourself drumming your fingers as you wait for a quick resolution to the challenges of everyday living, take a deep breath and ask God for patience. Remember that patience builds character . . . and the best moment to start building is this one.

SOMETHING TO THINK ABOUT

The best things in life seldom happen overnight; they usually take time. Henry Blackaby writes, "The grass that is here today and gone tomorrow does not require much time to mature. A big oak tree that lasts for generations requires much more time to grow and mature. God is concerned about your life through eternity. Allow Him to take all the time He needs to shape you for His purposes. Larger assignments will require longer periods of preparation." How true.

When we read of the great Biblical leaders, we see that it was not uncommon for God to ask them to wait, not just a day or two, but for years, until God was ready for them to act.

Gloria Gaither

We must learn to wait. There is grace supplied to the one who waits.

Mrs. Charles E. Cowman

In all negotiations of difficulties, a man may not look to sow and reap at once. He must prepare his business and so ripen it by degrees.

Francis Bacon

By his wisdom, he orders his delays so that they prove to be far better than our hurries.

C. H. Spurgeon

Let God use times of waiting to mold and shape your character. Let God use those times to purify your life and make you into a clean vessel for His service.

Henry Blackaby and Claude King

More from God's Word

Be gentle to everyone, able to teach, and patient.

2 Timothy 2:23 HCSB

The result of righteousness will be peace; the effect of righteousness will be quiet confidence forever.

Isaiah 32:17 HCSB

But if we hope for what we do not see, we eagerly wait for it with patience.

Romans 8:25 HCSB

The Lord is good to those who wait for Him, to the person who seeks Him.

Lamentations 3:25 HCSB

Wait on the LORD; be of good courage, and He shall strengthen your heart; wait, I say, on the LORD!

Psalm 27:14 NKJV

My Thoughts on This Lesson

_____

_____

_____

_____

_____

_____

_____

_____

_____

_____

A Prayer

Heavenly Father, let me wait quietly for You. Let me live
according to Your plan and according to Your timetable.
When I am hurried, slow me down. When I become impatient
with others, give me empathy. Today, I want to be a patient
Christian, Dear Lord, as I trust in You and in Your master plan.

Amen

Lesson 28

Money: Tool or Master?

The borrower is a slave to the lender.

Proverbs 22:7 HCSB

THE LESSON

Money is a helpful servant but a terrible master. So, you should manage money wisely.

The content of your character is demonstrated by the way you choose to spend money. If you spend money wisely, and if you give God His fair share, then you're doing just fine. But if you're up to your eyeballs in debt, and if "shop 'til you drop" is your unofficial motto, it's time to retire the credit cards and rearrange your priorities.

Our society is in love with money and the things that money can buy. God is not. God cares about people, not possessions, and so must we. We must, to the best of our abilities, love our neighbors as ourselves, and we must, to the best of our abilities, resist the mighty temptation to place possessions ahead of people.

> When you worry about what you don't have, you won't be able to enjoy what you do have.
>
> —
>
> *Charles Swindoll*

Money, in and of itself, is not evil; worshipping money is. So today, as you prioritize matters of importance for you and yours, remember that God is almighty, but the dollar is not.

Are you choosing to make money your master? If so, it's time to turn your thoughts and your prayers to more important matters. And, it's time to begin storing up riches that will endure throughout eternity: the spiritual kind.

SOMETHING TO THINK ABOUT

Put God where He belongs—first: Any relationship that doesn't honor God is a relationship that is destined for problems—and that includes your relationship with money. So spend (and save) accordingly.

Servants of God are always more concerned about ministry than money.

Rick Warren

If you want to be truly happy, you won't find it on an endless quest for more stuff. You'll find it in receiving God's generosity and in passing that generosity along.

Bill Hybels

Sadly, family problems and even financial problems are seldom the real problem, but often the symptom of a weak or nonexistent value system.

Dave Ramsey

The cross is laid on every Christian. It begins with the call to abandon the attachments of this world.

Dietrich Bonhoeffer

No man can stand in front of Jesus Christ and say "I want to make money."

Oswald Chambers

Your priorities, passions, goals, and fears are shown clearly in the flow of your money.

Dave Ramsey

There is no correlation between wealth and happiness.

Larry Burkett

Greed is enslaving. The more you have, the more you want—until eventually avarice consumes you.

Kay Arthur

Many things I have tried to grasp and have lost. That which I have placed in God's hands I still have.

Martin Luther

More from God's Word

For the love of money is a root of all kinds of evil, and by craving it, some have wandered away from the faith and pierced themselves with many pains.

1 Timothy 6:10 HCSB

Based on the gift they have received, everyone should use it to serve others, as good managers of the varied grace of God.

1 Peter 4:10 HCSB

Your life should be free from the love of money. Be satisfied with what you have, for He Himself has said, I will never leave you or forsake you.

Hebrews 13:5 HCSB

No one can be a slave of two masters, since either he will hate one and love the other, or be devoted to one and despise the other. You cannot be slaves of God and of money.

Matthew 6:24 HCSB

The one who loves money is never satisfied with money, and whoever loves wealth [is] never [satisfied] with income. This too is futile.

Ecclesiastes 5:10 HCSB

MY THOUGHTS ON THIS LESSON

A PRAYER

Dear Lord, help make me a responsible steward of
my financial resources. Let me trust Your Holy Word,
and let me use my tithe for the support of Your church
and for the eternal glory of Your Son. Amen

Lesson 29

Walking with the Wise

So follow the way of good people,
and keep to the paths of the righteous.
Proverbs 2:20 HCSB

THE LESSON

It pays to choose godly friends and wise mentors.

Do you wish to become wise? Then you must walk with people who, by their words and their presence, make you wiser. And, to the best of your ability, you must avoid those people who don't. That means that you must choose wise friends and mentors.

A savvy mentor can help you make character-building choices. And just as importantly, a thoughtful mentor can help you recognize and avoid the hidden big-time mistakes that can derail your day (or your life).

Wise mentors aren't really very hard to find if you look in the right places (but they're almost impossible to find if you look in the wrong places!). So today, select from your friends and family members a mentor whose judgment you trust. Then listen carefully to your mentor's advice and be willing to accept that advice even if accepting it requires effort, or pain, or both. Consider your mentor to be God's gift to you. Thank God for that gift, and use it.

SOMETHING TO THINK ABOUT

Rely on the advice of trusted friends and mentors. Proverbs 1:5 makes it clear: "A wise man will hear and increase learning, and a man of understanding will attain wise counsel" (NKJV). Do you want to be wise? Seek counsel from wise people, starting today.

The next best thing to being wise oneself is to live in a circle of those who are.

C. S. Lewis

The best times in life are made a thousand times better when shared with a dear friend.

Luci Swindoll

It takes a wise person to give good advice, but an even wiser person to take it.

Marie T. Freeman

In friendship, God opens your eyes to the glories of Himself.

Joni Eareckson Tada

Yes, the Spirit was sent to be our Counselor. Yes, Jesus speaks to us personally. But often he works through another human being.

John Eldredge

God often keeps us on the path by guiding us through the counsel of friends and trusted spiritual advisors.

Bill Hybels

The effective mentor strives to help a man or woman discover what they can be in Christ and then holds them accountable to become that person.

Howard Hendricks

Though I know intellectually how vulnerable I am to pride and power, I am the last one to know when I succumb to their seduction. That's why spiritual Lone Rangers are so dangerous—and why we must depend on trusted brothers and sisters who love us enough to tell us the truth.

Chuck Colson

The glory of friendship is not the outstretched hand, or the kindly smile, or the joy of companionship. It is the spiritual inspiration that comes to one when he discovers that someone else believes in him and is willing to trust him with his friendship.

Corrie ten Boom

The man who never reads will never be read; he who never quotes will never be quoted. He who will not use the thoughts of other men's brains proves that he has no brains of his own.

C. H. Spurgeon

More from God's Word

It is better to be criticized by a wise person than to be praised by a fool!

Ecclesiastes 7:5 NLT

A wise man will listen and increase his learning, and a discerning man will obtain guidance.

Proverbs 1:5 HCSB

My brothers, if any among you strays from the truth, and someone turns him back, he should know that whoever turns a sinner from the error of his way will save his life from death and cover a multitude of sins.

James 5:19-20 HCSB

The way of a fool is right in his own eyes, but he who heeds counsel is wise.

Proverbs 12:15 NKJV

The one who walks with the wise will become wise, but a companion of fools will suffer harm.

Proverbs 13:20 HCSB

MY THOUGHTS ON THIS LESSON

_____

_____

_____

_____

_____

_____

_____

_____

_____

A PRAYER

Dear Lord, thank You for family members, for friends, and for
mentors. When I am troubled, let me turn to them for help,
for guidance, for comfort, and for perspective. And Father,
let me be a friend and mentor to others, so that my love for You
may be reflected in my genuine concern for them. Amen

Lesson 30

Ask Him

The Lord is far from the wicked,
but He hears the prayer of the righteous.

Proverbs 15:29 HCSB

THE LESSON

God hears your prayers. Ask Him for the things you need.

How often do you ask God for His help and His wisdom? Occasionally? Intermittently? Whenever you experience a crisis? Hopefully not. Hopefully, you've acquired the habit of asking for God's assistance early and often. And hopefully, you have learned to seek His guidance in every aspect of your life.

Jesus made it clear to His disciples: they should petition God to meet their needs. So should you. Genuine, heartfelt prayer produces powerful changes in you and in your world. When you lift your heart to God, you open yourself to a never-ending source of divine wisdom and infinite love.

James 5:16 makes a promise that God intends to keep: when you pray earnestly, fervently, and often, great things will happen.

> We get into trouble when we think we know what to do and we stop asking God if we're doing it.
>
> —
>
> *Stormie Omartian*

Too many people, however, are too timid or too pessimistic to ask God to do big things. Please don't count yourself among their number.

God can do great things through you if you have the courage to ask Him (and the determination to keep asking Him). But don't expect Him to do all the work. When you do your part, He will do His part—and when He does, you can expect miracles to happen.

The Bible promises that God will guide you if you let Him. Your job is to let Him. But sometimes, you will be tempted to do otherwise. Sometimes, you'll be tempted to go along with the crowd; other times, you'll be tempted to do things your way, not God's way. When you feel those temptations, resist them.

God has promised that when you ask for His help, He will not withhold it. So ask. Ask Him to meet the needs of your day. Ask Him to lead you, to protect you, and to correct you. Then, trust the answers He gives.

God stands at the door and waits. When you knock, He opens. When you ask, He answers. Your task, of course, to make God a full partner in every aspect of your life—and to seek His guidance prayerfully, confidently, and often.

SOMETHING TO THINK ABOUT

Today, think of a specific need that is weighing heavily on your heart. Then, spend a few quiet moments asking God for His guidance and for His help.

We honor God by asking for great things when they are a part of His promise. We dishonor Him and cheat ourselves when we ask for molehills where He has promised mountains.

Vance Havner

When you ask God to do something, don't ask timidly; put your whole heart into it.

Marie T. Freeman

When there is a matter that requires definite prayer, pray until you believe God and until you can thank Him for His answer.

Hannah Whitall Smith

All we have to do is to acknowledge our need, move from self-sufficiency to dependence, and ask God to become our hiding place.

Bill Hybels

True prayer is measured by weight, not by length. A single groan before God may have more fullness of prayer in it than a fine oration of great length.

C. H. Spurgeon

More from God's Word

You do not have because you do not ask.

James 4:2 HCSB

If you remain in Me and My words remain in you, ask whatever you want and it will be done for you.

John 15:7 HCSB

What father among you, if his son asks for a fish, will, instead of a fish, give him a snake? Or if he asks for an egg, will give him a scorpion? If you then, who are evil, know how to give good gifts to your children, how much more will the heavenly Father give the Holy Spirit to those who ask Him?

Luke 11:11-13 HCSB

So I say to you, keep asking, and it will be given to you. Keep searching, and you will find. Keep knocking, and the door will be opened to you.

Luke 11:9 HCSB

Don't worry about anything, but in everything, through prayer and petition with thanksgiving, let your requests be made known to God.

Philippians 4:6 HCSB

My Thoughts on This Lesson

_____

_____

_____

_____

_____

_____

_____

_____

_____

A Prayer

Lord, today I will ask You for the things I need. In every situation,
I will come to You in prayer. You know what I want, Lord,
and more importantly, You know what I need. Yet even though
I know that You know, I still won't be too timid—
or too busy—to ask. Amen

More from God's Word

Accepting Christ

For God loved the world in this way: He gave His only Son, so that everyone who believes in Him will not perish but have eternal life.

John 3:16 HCSB

Yet we know that no one is justified by the works of the law but by faith in Jesus Christ. And we have believed in Christ Jesus, so that we might be justified by faith in Christ and not by the works of the law, because by the works of the law no human being will be justified.

Galatians 2:16 HCSB

Whoever believes that Jesus is the Christ is born of God, and everyone who loves Him who begot also loves him who is begotten of Him.

1 John 5:1 NKJV

God wanted to make known to those among the Gentiles the glorious wealth of this mystery, which is Christ in you, the hope of glory.

Colossians 1:27 HCSB

And we have seen and testify
that the Father has sent the Son
as Savior of the world.

—

1 John 4:14 NKJV

Christ's Sacrifice

For Christ also died for sins once for all, the just for the unjust, so that He might bring us to God, having been put to death in the flesh, but made alive in the spirit.

1 Peter 3:18 NASB

Everyone has to die once, then face the consequences. Christ's death was also a one-time event, but it was a sacrifice that took care of sins forever. And so, when he next appears, the outcome for those eager to greet him is, precisely, salvation.

Hebrews 9:27-28 MSG

For when we were still without strength, in due time Christ died for the ungodly.

Romans 5:6 NKJV

But God demonstrates His own love toward us, in that while we were still sinners, Christ died for us.

Romans 5:8 NKJV

Blessings

You will show me the path of life; in Your presence is fullness of joy; at Your right hand are pleasures forevermore.

Psalm 16:11 NKJV

I will make them and the area around My hill a blessing: I will send down showers in their season—showers of blessing.

Ezekiel 34:26 HCSB

Obey My voice, and I will be your God, and you shall be my people. And walk in all the ways that I have commanded you, that it may be well with you.

Jeremiah 7:23 NKJV

The Lord bless you and keep you; the Lord make His face shine upon you, and be gracious to you.

Numbers 6:24-25 NKJV

Blessed is a man who endures trials, because when he passes the test he will receive the crown of life that He has promised to those who love Him.

James 1:12 HCSB

Adversity

When you are in distress and all these things have happened to you, you will return to the Lord your God in later days and obey Him. He will not leave you, destroy you, or forget the covenant with your fathers that He swore to them by oath, because the Lord your God is a compassionate God.

Deuteronomy 4:30-31 HCSB

Whatever has been born of God conquers the world. This is the victory that has conquered the world: our faith.

1 John 5:4 HCSB

Dear friends, when the fiery ordeal arises among you to test you, don't be surprised by it, as if something unusual were happening to you. Instead, as you share in the sufferings of the Messiah rejoice, so that you may also rejoice with great joy at the revelation of His glory.

1 Peter 4:12-13 HCSB

We are pressured in every way but not crushed; we are perplexed but not in despair.

2 Corinthians 4:8 HCSB

I called to the Lord in my distress;
I called to my God.
From His temple He heard my voice.
—

2 Samuel 22:7 HCSB

Evil

Therefore, submit to God. But resist the Devil, and he will flee from you. Draw near to God, and He will draw near to you. Cleanse your hands, sinners, and purify your hearts, double-minded people!

James 4:7-8 HCSB

Do not be conquered by evil, but conquer evil with good.

Romans 12:21 HCSB

For everyone who practices wicked things hates the light and avoids it, so that his deeds may not be exposed. But anyone who lives by the truth comes to the light, so that his works may be shown to be accomplished by God.

John 3:20–21 HCSB

He replied, "Every plant that My heavenly Father didn't plant will be uprooted."

Matthew 15:13 HCSB

But the path of the just is like the shining sun, that shines ever brighter unto the perfect day. The way of the wicked is like darkness; they do not know what makes them stumble.

Proverbs 4:18-19 NKJV

Don't consider yourself to be wise;
fear the Lord
and turn away from evil.

—

Proverbs 3:7 HCSB

Fearing God

The fear of the Lord is the beginning of knowledge, but fools despise wisdom and instruction.

Proverbs 1:7 NKJV

The fear of the Lord is the beginning of wisdom, and the knowledge of the Holy One is understanding.

Proverbs 9:10 HCSB

The fear of the Lord is the beginning of wisdom; all who follow His instructions have good insight.

Psalm 111:10 HCSB

The fear of the Lord is a fountain of life, turning people from the snares of death.

Proverbs 14:27 HCSB

To fear the Lord is to hate evil.

—

Proverbs 8:13 HCSB

God's Presence

Draw near to God, and He will draw near to you.

James 4:8 HCSB

You will seek Me and find Me when you search for Me with all your heart.

Jeremiah 29:13 HCSB

The Lord is near all who call out to Him, all who call out to Him with integrity. He fulfills the desires of those who fear Him; He hears their cry for help and saves them.

Psalm 145:18-19 HCSB

Surely goodness and mercy shall follow me all the days of my life: and I will dwell in the house of the Lord for ever.

Psalm 23:6 KJV

I am not alone, because the Father is with Me.

John 16:32 HCSB

Putting God First

You shall have no other gods before Me.

Exodus 20:3 NKJV

Be careful not to forget the Lord.

Deuteronomy 6:12 HCSB

It is good to give thanks to the Lord, and to sing praises to Your name, O Most High; to declare Your lovingkindness in the morning, and Your faithfulness every night.

Psalm 92:1-2 NKJV

Love the Lord your God with all your heart, with all your soul, and with all your strength.

Deuteronomy 6:5 HCSB

The Devil said to Him, "I will give You their splendor and all this authority, because it has been given over to me, and I can give it to anyone I want. If You, then, will worship me, all will be Yours." And Jesus answered him, "It is written: You shall worship the Lord your God, and Him alone you shall serve."

Luke 4:6-8 HCSB

Happiness

How happy are those whose way is blameless, who live according to the law of the Lord! Happy are those who keep His decrees and seek Him with all their heart.

Psalm 119:1-2 HCSB

If they serve Him obediently, they will end their days in prosperity and their years in happiness.

Job 36:11 HCSB

The one who understands a matter finds success, and the one who trusts in the Lord will be happy.

Proverbs 16:20 HCSB

Happy are the people whose strength is in You, whose hearts are set on pilgrimage.

Psalm 84:5 HCSB

How happy is the man who does not follow the advice of the wicked, or take the path of sinners, or join a group of mockers!

Psalm 1:1 HCSB

A joyful heart is good medicine,
but a broken spirit
dries up the bones.

—

Proverbs 17:22 HCSB

Abundance

And God is able to make every grace overflow to you, so that in every way, always having everything you need, you may excel in every good work.

2 Corinthians 9:8 HCSB

Until now you have asked for nothing in My name. Ask and you will receive, that your joy may be complete.

John 16:24 HCSB

Come to terms with God and be at peace; in this way good will come to you.

Job 22:21 HCSB

My cup runs over. Surely goodness and mercy shall follow me all the days of my life; and I will dwell in the house of the Lord forever.

Psalm 23:5-6 NKJV

And He said to them, "Take heed and beware of covetousness, for one's life does not consist in the abundance of the things he possesses."

Luke 12:15 NKJV

I have come that they may have life, and that they may have it more abundantly.

—

John 10:10 NKJV

*Trust in the Lord with all
your heart, and do not rely on
your own understanding;
think about Him in all your ways,
and He will guide you
on the right paths.*

—

Proverbs 3:5-6 HCSB